Cornerstones for Writing

Teacher's Book
Year 5

Alison Green, Jill Hurlstone
and Diane Skipper

Series Editor
Jean Glasberg

CAMBRIDGE
UNIVERSITY PRESS

Contents

Introduction

'Write about something you did in the holidays.' As most teachers know, this kind of instruction usually leads to uninspiring results: unstructured writing with no clear beginning or ending, which is often repetitive or a mix of fact and fantasy. Even worse, it can lead to blank sheets of paper and demoralised children. *Cornerstones for Writing* provides both teacher and children with the guidance they need to proceed step by step, with confidence, to a written text. It fully supports the writing objectives in the National Literacy Strategy.

In many classrooms, excellent work is being done to help children write fluently and effectively. However, for all too many children, success in writing continues to trail significantly behind that in reading. This resource aims to narrow the gap between reading and writing ability in a number of ways:

- by providing carefully selected texts as models, so that children learn the benefits of reading as authors and writing as readers;
- by helping children to identify key structural and linguistic features of important text types;
- by taking children step by step through the processes used by successful writers;
- by motivating children through establishing a clear audience and purpose for writing.

Cornerstones for Writing components

The resource has the following components:

Writing Models OHT Pack *or* Poster Pack

The OHT pack contains 32 overhead transparencies, which can be used with any overhead projector to display texts to the whole class. As an alternative, the same material is available in a poster pack of 16 double-sided A1 posters, in a 'write-on-wipe-off' format. Both the OHT pack and poster pack comprise:

- example texts from a variety of sources, which provide models for each of the different types of writing covered within the resource;
- versions of planning frameworks which appear in the copymasters, allowing the teacher to model planning with the whole class;
- where appropriate, activities for the whole class which draw attention to particular features of writing.

Notes on how to use each OHT or poster can be found in the instructions for each session within this teacher's book.

Teacher's Book

The teacher's book contains:

- notes to help you conduct the shared sessions for each step of the writing process; these are arranged in six units of work, covering the year;
- summaries of the group or independent follow-up activities, most of which are set out in the pupil's book (see below);
- suggestions for a guided focus for each group session ('guided group support');
- photocopy masters for group work;
- homework suggestions to support each unit;
- self-assessment sheets to allow children to evaluate their success with each unit;
- facsimiles of the text extracts in the OHT pack/poster pack, to help your planning.

Pupil's Book

The pupil's book provides activities to follow up and reinforce the teaching in the shared sessions. Most of these activities relate to the early stages of the writing process (i.e. Modelling – see below), as once the writing is well under way the children will be focusing on their own compositions.

Key to symbols

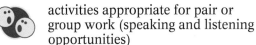

red	activities appropriate for the less able child
blue	activities appropriate for the average child
yellow	activities appropriate for the more able child
	activities appropriate for pair or group work (speaking and listening opportunities)

Five steps to writing

For children to write confidently, they need to be taught a generic procedure which they can apply to <u>any</u> writing task. The *Cornerstones for Writing* five-step process helps young authors to approach their writing just as a skilled adult would. These five steps are outlined below:

1 Modelling

This step provides children with a successful 'how to' model for constructing their own text. Using the appropriate model text(s) from the OHT or poster pack, you should demonstrate how to map out a structural framework and identify linguistic features. Subsequent group activities encourage the children to remember and use this model for their own future writing.

2 Planning

Planning is an excellent method of establishing and keeping control. If children know how to plan in detail, and have practised the skill frequently enough for it to become familiar, they are likely to write more effectively.

Planning frameworks are helpful for children of most ages and abilities, especially when using one that has been problem-solved in class from a model text. Over a number of units, the children will learn the generic skill of 'finding' a suitable framework for writing and then using it to organise content. This is much more useful than becoming over-reliant on published 'writing frames', which, when used without real understanding on the part of the children, may leave some to flounder when the frame is taken away.

3 Drafting

Drafting is the process of getting words and ideas down on paper in provisional form, without worrying too much about elegance of expression or organisation of the pages. With the planning already done, the children are free to concentrate on the writing itself.

4 Revising and editing

Revising focuses on the content and style of a text, and allows the children to check that they have written everything that needed to be written, and are satisfied with it. It also provides an opportunity to evaluate the text from the viewpoint of the intended reader, and make any changes necessary to address the reader's needs. Editing focuses on accurate spelling and punctuation, to ensure effective communication of the author's ideas to the reader.

This step usually requires the most diplomatic handling by the teacher. The children have worked hard to produce their texts, and sometimes fail to see the point of doing any more work. It is very important, therefore, to show how improvements can be made. This will be facilitated by frequent reading and re-reading aloud to bring out 'before and after' contrasts. A really successful shared experience of revising and editing will often convert young writers away from a haphazard 'one-go' approach.

5 Publishing

Publishing is the final step in the process, where the text is produced in the form in which it will reach its intended audience. This may be done by, for example, the posting of a letter, the performance of a poem or the creation of an attractive classroom display. At this stage the arrangement of words on pages and the inclusion of illustrations, diagrams and other displayed material become most important.

Ensuring that the finished text reaches its intended audience in polished form validates the whole process. Even under great pressure of time, teachers ignore this at their peril! If the children's work never reaches an audience beyond their teacher, it is hardly surprising that they do not become audience-aware, and do not learn to craft texts for a variety of audiences and purposes. Young writers are often inspired by the pride and success they feel when they see their work word-processed, or neatly copied and displayed.

Teaching the five steps
Modelling
Conducting a shared modelling session

The nature of a shared modelling session is specific to each different text type, so much more detailed guidance is given in the shared session notes for each unit.

Modelling in group work

The children use a range of activities in the pupil's book and, where appropriate, on copymasters to familiarise themselves with the structure and features of the text type.

Planning
Conducting a shared planning session

Before the writing begins, it is essential that children know for whom they are writing, why they are writing, and how the outcome of their work will be 'published'. Where possible, share these decisions with the children to enhance motivation. Give them a deadline for producing the texts, tell them how much time and support will be available and whether they should write individually, in pairs or in groups.

Purpose and audience are crucial to the content, tone and length of the final document. Spend some time discussing and considering the needs of the audience: make preliminary decisions about how complicated the vocabulary can be, how formal the tone should be, etc.

Establish the intended method of publication. (This is for the children's independent writing – although the class text could also be published if you wish.) For example, the finished writing could be:

- made into a booklet for younger children;
- published in the school magazine;
- made into a classroom display;
- typed up as a letter to a specific recipient;
- read out in assembly.

Make brief notes of your decisions on these issues and keep them on display to refer back to during the writing process. Plan the shared text together with the children and, similarly, display the class plan as a model for their own plans.

Planning in group work

The children follow the same procedure as in the shared session, and plan their own texts. They work from either planning frameworks on copymasters or prompts in the pupil's book. It may be helpful to conduct a guided group session for this step with the less able children. This will ensure that they have a firm basis to work from once drafting begins (see **Guided focus suggestions** on page 10).

Drafting

Conducting a shared drafting session

It is strongly recommended that drafts be written on large sheets of paper so they can be kept for subsequent revising, and examined again alongside the finished text. It is often helpful for children to see the entire 'evolution' of a piece of writing.

Especially in their early experiences, it is difficult for young writers to be disciplined enough to stick to a plan. Read back each section of planning notes to the children as you go along and involve them in composing sentences to build and elaborate the text. Keep them firmly on track by referring repeatedly to what they have already decided to do, rejecting suggestions that would move away from this. (Occasionally, however, you may wish to add in an inspired 'extra' to make the point that, although planning is a very useful procedure, texts are not set in stone until published.)

Drafting may sometimes be slow to gain momentum – you may need to suggest some alternatives for discussion. Children often love to vote on the best choice from a number of strong suggestions. Good ideas which are not used in the shared text can be used in the children's own writing.

When drafting, do not worry about some sentences being too informal, or about words that do not quite fit – you need some material for improving in the revising and editing step. Often, if there are too many conflicting ideas, or if the children are becoming bogged down in how to write a particular part of the text, it is best to scribble something provisional and move on quickly. Problems can be underlined and returned to later. Often the solution to a writing problem becomes clearer as the text progresses.

Keep reading the text back to the children so that they establish a 'feel' for its tone and flow. Young writers often need to hear their writing read aloud in order to appreciate fully its length, sentence structure, etc.

'Time out' discussions may help to promote the full involvement of all the children during shared sessions. The use of small wipe-off boards for children to write and show their contributions may overcome any reluctance to speak aloud. It may also help to maintain pace in a lesson – especially if the children can be kept thinking and writing while you scribe an agreed sentence.

Finally, remember that the teacher is in charge of the shared text! Do not be afraid to 'drive' or control the piece to make a point or fulfil an objective. Explain and discuss how you are thinking as you work. As children gain in experience and confidence you will undoubtedly wish to involve them more collaboratively at times, but shared writing remains the main vehicle for teacher demonstration of writing skills.

Drafting in group work

It is often a good idea for the children to work in pairs and to tell their partner what they intend to write before writing it down. Verbalising their thoughts first can help the writing process and deters the children from making assumptions about the knowledge of the reader. Their partner will inevitably ask 'Why?', 'How?' and 'When?' if things are not clear to them.

It may be helpful to conduct a guided group session for this step with the less able or average children. These children will need some support with 'getting the language flowing' for a specific text type or audience (see **Guided focus suggestions** on page 10).

Revising and editing

Conducting a shared revising and editing session

Display the first draft. Discuss its effectiveness in relation to the main features of the text type, the original purpose for writing, the intended audience and so on. Praise its strengths, but be realistic about any problems or weaknesses. Remind the children that even professional authors have to revise and edit their work in order to make it worth publishing.

Straight away, deal with any parts of the text that were marked 'to come back to' while the first draft was being written. Use a new colour of pen so that changes are obvious. Next, ask the children to check the class plan and any additional materials (such as posters made in previous sessions) to ensure that the content includes everything that was planned. Discuss whether any additional content is needed at this stage. Then examine the style, flow and tone of the text. Decide whether the right words have been used, and whether any sentences need to be altered.

Sometimes a class will stoutly deny that there are any improvements to be made. Be prepared with two or three points that you are going to insist that they address. Also, be prepared to suggest some alternative improvements for them to evaluate and select from. Gradually, as they gain faith in this part of the process, the children will become more enthusiastic and discerning in their contributions.

You should also consider how well the text addresses the needs of its intended audience. Encourage the class to pretend that they are reading the work for the first time, 'in role' as members of this audience. Help the children to appreciate that a piece of writing is effective only if the intended audience can read or understand it.

Make a final check of spelling and grammar. Decide beforehand, according to your teaching objectives, how much responsibility you expect the children to take for ensuring the final standard of correctness in the shared text. Often it will be you, as scribe, who automatically assumes most editorial responsibility. Having made any necessary teaching points, remaining corrections should not take up too much time.

It can sometimes be very useful to use one of the children's drafts for a shared revision session. Children are often pleased that their work is being held up as an example (it is, of course, important to praise the work before revising and editing begins). Type out the child's work in advance, correcting any spelling, punctuation or other errors that are not to be part of the revising focus.

Revising and editing in group work

In groups, children 'echo' the revising and editing process, as for the other steps. It may be helpful to give them a checklist of questions that they can work through in pairs. For example:

- Is the language right for a report (or whatever text type is being written)?
- Are the information and the language right for your audience?
- Read your text to your partner. Is there anything that doesn't sound right?
- Have you checked the spelling, punctuation and grammar?

It is often useful to give children a <u>very specific</u>

focus for their revising and editing, and then ask them to work on this in pairs. One way the children can do this is to swap texts, and 'mark' their partner's work with some useful suggestions based on the given focus, using a different coloured pen. They then pass back the text, explain their suggestions and work together on improving the text.

It may be helpful to conduct a guided group session for this step with the more able children. They often learn best when spotting weaknesses in their own work and considering a range of possible improvements (see **Guided focus suggestions** on page 10).

Publishing

Conducting a shared publishing session

Time pressures will mean that it is easier to 'publish' some shared texts than others. Where it would be difficult to publish a complete version, pick out instances in the shared text which could benefit from presentational changes.

Remind the children of the intended audience, and any needs or preferences this audience may have. Revise the original purpose for writing, and consider how both of these factors have dictated the form the text has taken. Try to evaluate the impact the text will have on its intended audience.

Discuss the layout of the text. Identify ways in which its presentation could support the content. For instance, clarity of information in a report text could be enhanced through the use of a main title and headings, together with an annotated diagram, or a story could be illustrated in an attractive and informative way. Consider different ways of positioning the illustrations, rather than simply having the text at the top and a picture at the bottom. For example, split the text with the illustration in the middle, or put the text in a column with pictures down the side or decorative borders around the edge.

Discuss briefly the relative merits of highlighting effects such as bold, underlining, italics, enlarged font, changed font, upper case, etc. Decide how to present the title and headings.

Decide on the necessary publication methods and materials. These could include the use of a computer to produce the finished text, or some good handwriting pens and some attractively coloured paper. Using very simple paper-folding techniques, attractive 'books' can be made for the presentation of shorter texts. Despite their simplicity these often encourage children to produce outstanding results.

Publishing in group work

Once again, children can 'echo' the publishing ideas discussed and tried out in the shared session. When the children work on the 'best' copy of their work, it is a good opportunity to consider the importance of clear handwriting and good spelling.

Do everything possible to involve the children in presenting their finished texts to the intended audience, whether this entails them reading their stories to another class, performing their work in school assemblies or producing questionnaires asking other children what they think of work on display in the corridors.

How to plan with *Cornerstones for Writing*

In each year there are six units, corresponding roughly to six half-terms. Each *Cornerstones for Writing* unit takes one text type as its main focus, based on NLS requirements.

It is recommended that each unit be covered over a two-week period of concentrated, writing-focused work, as follows:

Week 1: reading linked to writing;
Week 2: writing.

To accommodate this in the teaching programme, reading and writing objectives for a chosen text type can be <u>blocked</u> together and given a heavier-than-average weighting of teaching time. This can include both literacy hour time and 'other English' time. Most teachers would agree that time beyond the literacy hour is essential in order to fulfil the requirement to teach extended and developed writing. Any remaining NLS writing objectives for each half term are covered in the 'additional sessions' (see below) which follow each unit.

Half term	
Week 1	Work on NLS range of texts
Week 2	for term and (mainly) reading
Week 3	objectives
	Cornerstones for Writing
Week 4	Reading linked to writing
Week 5	Writing
Week 6	As for Weeks 1–3

Each unit leads to the production of developed texts on two levels:

1 by the whole class, done in shared sessions with you, the teacher;
2 by individuals or groups, independently or with your guidance.

Over the course of a unit, you will address and reinforce many text-, sentence- and word-level objectives for the term. Once each unit is under way, particularly in the latter stages of drafting, revising and editing, and publishing, you will probably need to 'flex' the structure of the literacy hour to allow for a 'writing workshop' approach.

Whole-class work could be devoted to shared planning or writing, but incorporating supportive sentence- or word-level focuses. Guided support could focus on scaffolding the children's own work as it progresses; independent sessions should allow time for the children to plan, draft and improve their work in the light of what they are learning about the target text type. However, if you wish to follow the classic structure of the literacy hour, a unit could even be followed through in quarter-hour stages, as long as the children's interest is maintained.

It is strongly recommended that plenary sessions be maintained, even where the literacy hour has been 'flexed', in order to sum up and reinforce the children's learning during the course of each writing lesson. In this way, the children discuss not only what they have done, but also <u>how</u> they have done it, and what they have learned about the writing process.

Linking reading and writing objectives

As reading and writing are inextricably linked and mutually supportive, every unit includes close reading analysis of simple model texts. However, it is also strongly recommended that each unit be immediately preceded by further reading experiences within the target text type, in accordance with NLS reading objectives. If, as the children read, they are helped to appreciate how an author has written the text with great care in a particular way and for a particular purpose, it is far more likely that they will be able to write successful texts of their own.

Using the additional sessions

As outlined above, *Cornerstones for Writing* focuses on one main text type per unit (therefore per half term), covering a great many of the writing objectives within the NLS framework. The 'additional sessions' will help you cover the few remaining objectives.

The additional sessions usually consist of a single shared session (or occasionally two or even three sessions) followed by group activities. This is because, assuming that the main text type has been taught in the way we suggest, you will probably plan to give these objectives 'light touch' treatment because of time limitations. However, the content of these sessions varies, and you should use your professional judgement in planning whether/when and how to use the following types of additional session:

- short, one-off tasks which could reasonably be achieved in a single literacy hour session (e.g. **Writing a poem about feelings** in unit 1);
- more broadly based objectives which you may wish to expand if time permits (e.g. **Writing from another character's point of view** in unit 5);

- useful skills work which could be slotted into the main two-week writing block if you feel the children are ready for it, or perhaps taught in a guided session to one ability group (e.g. **Writing up personal notes for others to read** in unit 4).

Special features of *Cornerstones for Writing*

Differentiation by colour coding

In *Cornerstones for Writing*, group follow-up activities are differentiated at three levels. Colour coding is used for this in the pupil's book and referred to in the teaching notes. The following coding is used:

- **red** to indicate activities appropriate for the less able child;
- **blue** to indicate activities appropriate for the average child;
- **yellow** to indicate activities appropriate for the more able child.

Guided focus suggestions (see below) are provided in the teacher's book for each session, with different suggestions for each of the red, blue and yellow groups. Additional differentiation can be achieved through the size and constitution of specific groupings. For example, less able or less prolific writers could be supported by allowing them to work collaboratively on one text, in pairs or groups. More able writers could be challenged to produce individual documents.

Guided focus suggestions

Group work allows small groups of children to use for themselves writing skills previously demonstrated and trialled in shared sessions. In guided group work, the demands on children's developing authorship can be carefully structured and focused by the teacher to ensure appropriate differentiation and maximum progress. The teaching notes in this book provide specific suggestions for guided group support at each stage, to help you to achieve this. However, it is of course vital to tailor your focus to the specific needs of the children in each group, which you are in the best position to assess and which no book can fully provide for.

Once writing workshops get under way (see **How to plan with *Cornerstones for Writing*** above) and the emphasis begins to shift from demonstration towards independent writing, you may choose to 'squeeze' the usual half hour of whole-class work down to twenty minutes (the plenary may also be contracted). This creates time for <u>two</u> guided group lessons during each workshop hour, meaning that each group has two teaching visits over the course of a week.

Speaking and listening symbol

Regardless of whether the children carry out their follow-up work individually, in pairs or in groups, it is important that they interact with one another. Specific opportunities for speaking and listening are emphasised in *Cornerstones for Writing* with a special symbol (two talking heads). This appears in the pupil's book next to relevant activities, and is repeated in the summary of activities in the teacher's book.

Structured or focused talk about writing is almost more important than the writing itself because it involves children in <u>thinking about how to write</u> and <u>transmitting ideas</u>. Although teachers sometimes worry that insufficient 'evidence' of writing activity may be produced, the finished texts at the end of each unit should reflect all the teaching and learning that have taken place.

Self-assessment sheets

Cornerstones for Writing encourages children to evaluate their own work and become aware of their progress. A simple self-assessment sheet is provided with each unit, which can be given to each child once they have completed their writing. The sheets may prove suitable for inclusion in records of achievement.

Homework

Many schools now provide regular homework for their pupils, so we include a variety of suggestions at the end of each unit. The suggestions are intended to reinforce the knowledge and skills gained in each unit, though they are not essential to the success of the writing project. To avoid any potential 'paperchase' problems – and to prevent marking overload! – many of the homework suggestions are based on research or involve reading or discussion.

Cross-curricular links

One of the main aims of the NLS is to promote the cross-curricular applications of literacy skills, rather than to teach them as simply 'English'. For instance, if the children are learning how to write reports, a real purpose for report-writing may be found in the science curriculum – the children could present, in a report, all the information they have learnt about materials, life processes, etc. Likewise, children can deploy their recount skills in history lessons, writing 'in role' as eyewitnesses to major events. You should seek cross-curricular links for writing projects wherever possible.

Clear opportunities for cross-curricular links with *Cornerstones for Writing* are highlighted in the teaching notes.

ICT opportunities

ICT will prove particularly valuable in recording, revising and editing class or individual texts. Word-processing offers a quick, easy way of finding and correcting mis-spellings or experimenting with the structure of sentences. Paragraphing, headings and the shape and size of layout can all be changed at the press of a button.

The internet used in researching information is also a powerful tool that can help children plan their writing. Where appropriate, opportunities for using the internet are clearly highlighted in *Cornerstones for Writing*.

Preparing for the National Tests (SATs)

Children will learn important writing skills in the course of their *Cornerstones for Writing* projects. These will stand them in good stead for tackling the full range of National Test writing tasks with confidence and effectiveness.

It is important for teachers and pupils to be aware that annual reports on children's performance in the writing tests commonly refer to:

- weaknesses in adapting text for different purposes and audiences, including choosing an appropriate text type and style;
- poor control over textual structure and balance – being able to select, sequence and shape events or ideas;
- problems using paragraphs accurately and appropriately;
- lack of writing 'stamina' – the tendency to lose control, slacken pace or 'dry up' before the end;
- weak or inappropriate endings, reflecting poor planning beforehand;
- poor sentence control – the ability to use and organise sentences of varying length and structure.

Teachers often feel that pupils perform at less than their best due to 'exam nerves' or through not knowing what examiners are looking for in response to particular questions. To help overcome this, *Cornerstones for Writing* provides a section entitled 'How to write answers to SATs questions' (teacher's book pp. 111–114, pupil's book pp. 75–79) which gives practice in this essential preparation.

We suggest that you use the materials provided as follows:

i   Choose a question from those offered in the pupil's book, and ask the children to read it carefully.

ii Children should work in pairs to identify the writing skills the question demands, before planning how best to construct their text. They should use the questions on page 75 of the pupil's book as a guide.

iii If you wish, ask each pair to compare their findings with another pair and come to an agreed plan of action.

iv Go through the 'answers' together as a class or group. You can use the completed tables on pages 111–114 of this book as a guide.

v   You <u>may</u> wish to ask the children to write full responses to the question. If so, remind them to show off all they have learnt about the particular text type, and emphasise the importance of sticking to their plans.

Note: this section contains facsimiles of OHTs/posters which do not also appear as copymasters.

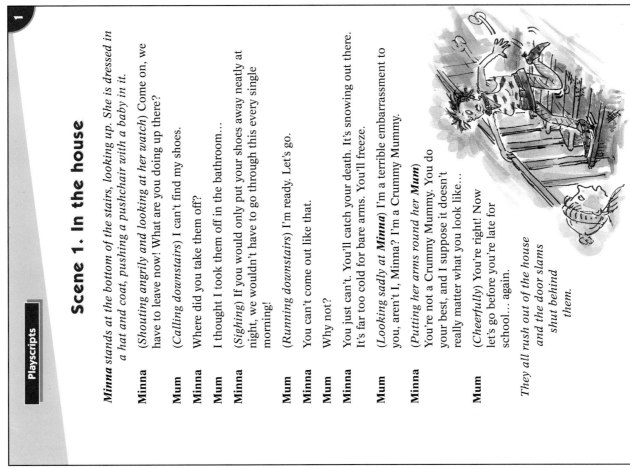

Note: this section contains facsimile of OHTs/posters which do not also appear as copymasters.

Playscripts

Extract from *Crummy Mummy and Me*

You don't exactly ask to get sick, do you? I mean, you don't go round *inviting* germs and viruses to move in and do their worst to your body. You don't actually *apply* for trembling legs and feeling shivery, and a head that's had a miniature steel band practising for a carnival in it all night. And if you should happen to mention to your own mother that you feel absolutely terrible, you would expect a bit of sympathy, wouldn't you?

I wouldn't. Not any more.

"You don't *look* very poorly."

That's what she said. And she said it suspiciously, too, as if I was one of those people who's always making excuses to stay off school and spend the day wrapped in a downie on the sofa watching Bagpuss and Playschool and Pebble Mill at One.

"Well, I feel absolutely rotten."

"You don't look it."

"I'm sorry!" I snapped. (I was getting pretty cross.) "Sorry I can't manage a bright-green face for you! Or purple spots on my belly! Or all my hair falling out! But I feel rotten just the same!"

From *Crummy Mummy and Me* by Anne Fine

Playscripts

Write in the dialogue and stage directions for Crusher. Think about his character.

Minna, Mum, Crusher and **the baby** *are in the sitting room.* **Mum** *and* **Crusher** *are watching a video.* **Minna** *is annoyed at* **Crusher** *for giving her baby sister sugary juice to drink.*

Minna   (*To* **Mum**) You really shouldn't let Crusher give that stuff to the baby.

Crusher   (   ) _____

Minna   It rots her teeth.

Crusher   (   ) _____

Minna   Drinking sugary juice is a terrible habit. You really shouldn't buy it.

Crusher   (   ) _____

Based on *Crummy Mummy and Me* by Anne Fine

Note: this section contains facsimile of OHTs/posters which do not also appear as copymasters.

7

Recount for different audiences

The Siege of Troy

Early in the twelfth century BC, a great conflict arose when the beautiful Helen, wife of King Menelaus of Sparta, fell in love with Paris, son of King Priam of Troy. She eloped with him to his father's palace, where the couple took shelter within the mighty walls of the rich city. As a result, the Greeks declared a war to avenge the insult to Menelaus.

When the Greek army arrived at Troy, they attacked bravely, but found its walls were so strong they could not capture the city. So began a siege that lasted for ten years. Eventually, the Greeks had the idea of building an enormous wooden horse. Soldiers were hidden inside, and the horse was left near the city gates. Next, the Greeks returned to their ships and pretended to sail away, to give the impression that they had retreated from the siege.

The Trojan lookouts watched their enemies sail away, then opened the city gates. The inhabitants rushed out to examine the offering left behind by the Greeks. They dragged it inside the city walls and began to celebrate a victorious end to the war.

Late that night the concealed soldiers crept out of the wooden horse, and slaughtered the guards on the walls. They unlocked the city gates, letting in the Greek army which burnt Troy and killed most of its people.

Paris was slain in the desperate battle and the Greeks seized Helen and carried her back to her husband. The great city of Troy was burned to the ground, and Menelaus was avenged at last.

6

Playscripts

Grandad

Grandad's dead
And I'm sorry about that.

He'd a huge black overcoat.
He felt proud in it.
You could have hidden
A football crowd in it.
Far too big –
It was a lousy fit
But Grandad didn't
Mind a bit.
He wore it all winter
With a squashed black hat.

Now he's dead
And I'm sorry about that.

He'd got twelve stories.
I'd heard every one of them
Hundreds of times
But that was the fun of them:
You knew what was coming
So you could join in.
He'd got big hands
And brown, grooved skin
And when he laughed
It knocked you flat.

Now he's dead
And I'm sorry about that.

Kit Wright, 'Grandad'

Note: this section contains facsimile of OHTs/posters which do not also appear as copymasters.

9

Recount for different audiences

Dear Nicias,

The siege of Troy is all over... and guess what? It's all down to me!

It all started last month when I took the wife to the market to buy her some new clothes. Everyone was talking about the siege that was dragging on for years at Troy. All this because Paris kidnapped some ugly old princess!

Back home, I gave my son a toy horse I'd bought at the market. Zeno is a strong little fellow (a chip off the old block) and soon broke off the horse's head. Then he found he could put things inside it and push the head back on.

My wife laughed. "That would be a great way to smuggle our hoplites into Troy!" Of course, she's only a woman, so she couldn't possibly have realised what she was saying. But being a superior male, I came up with a great plan.

Our soldiers would build an enormous wooden horse and leave it outside Troy, then row their ships out of sight. The Trojans would think the horse was a gift from a retreating army. They would then take the horse into the city, not realising that our hoplites were hidden inside! At night, our boys would sneak out and open the city gates. In would surge the Greek army, having rowed back again under cover of darkness. Troy would be defeated.

And, as you now know... it worked! I'm a genius, a great military adviser! I wonder what my next great contribution to world history might be?

All the best, mate

Diogenes

8

Recount for different audiences

GREEKS MAKE HAY AS TROJANS WHINE

When Paris, Prince of Troy, ran off with beautiful Princess Helen of Greece, he couldn't have made a worse mistake. King "Angry" Agamemnon sent his entire fleet to get her back.

The face that launched a thousand ships

"We besieged Troy for ten years and lost a lot of good men," said Angry at a press conference yesterday. "We were at our wits' end. But then we came up with the winning tactic. We pretended to run away and leave them a large wooden horse by way of saying sorry."

"Just what we always wanted!" thought the Trojans. They saw the Greeks had gone, and dragged the horse into town. But what they didn't realise was that the Greeks had only run away behind the nearest hill and that the horse was hollow and filled with elite troops.

When night fell the soldiers crept out of the horse, seized the town and opened the gates to let the Greek army in. They massacred half the Trojan population and turned the rest into slaves. The only Trojan who managed to escape was a warrior named Aeneas.

Note: this section contains facsimile of OHTs/posters which do not also appear as copymasters.

13

Legends

Odysseus and the Cyclops

Long, long ago, Odysseus and his men set sail after fighting in a terrible war. They were going home at last.

After sailing across lonely seas for many days, they realised with dismay that their food and water supplies were running low. They needed to find land soon or they would die. At last they heard a shout, "Land!"

In the distance they could see an island. They decided to land and look for food.

As they drew nearer, they saw towering cliffs pitted with gigantic caves, and fields of sheep as large as buffaloes.

They scrambled ashore and climbed a rocky path up to the nearest cave. Suddenly the ground began to shake. Something big was approaching.

Into the cave stomped a man as big as a mountain. His enormous mouth was like a dark, evil-smelling cave and in the centre of his forehead glared a single massive eye like a giant pebble. It was the Cyclops, Polyphemus.

As the Cyclops rolled a massive boulder across the cave entrance he noticed the Greeks cowering in a corner. He laughed loudly. His laugh was like a great crack of thunder and the Greeks trembled with fear. Then, reaching out, he grabbed two of the men and tossed them into his cavernous mouth.

From *The Adventures of Odysseus* by Geraldine McCaughrean

12

Recount for different audiences

Alexander and the Hellenistic age

In the fourth century BC, a strong-looking man called Philip II turned Macedonia into one of the most powerful states in Greece. After his assassination in 337 BC, his 20-year-old son Alexander, a military genius, took over the reins of power.

Not content with ruling Greece, Alexander invaded Persian territory in 334 BC, and then pressed on through Asia Minor, then south and east to Egypt, Afghanistan and India. He established new Greek cities, such as Alexandria in Egypt, and therefore spread Greek culture over a vast area. Alexander, called 'the Great', intended to create a huge empire, incorporating most of the then known world. His death from a fever in 323 BC ended this ambition, and, instead, his vast empire was divided up among his family and generals.

From the death of Alexander until about 30 BC is known as the 'Hellenistic age' from the word 'Hellene', meaning Greek. The Hellenistic kingdoms preserved many aspects of Greek life that were eventually overcome by the rising power of Rome.

From *Ancient Greece*, reproduced by permission of Dorling Kindersley

Note: this section contains facsimile of OHTs/posters which do not also appear as copymasters.

15

Legends

Beginning Hero/heroine		
Extraordinary character		
Setting		
Problem		
Middle Events		
Climax		
End Resolution		
Conclusion		

14

Legends

"My plan has only just begun," said Odysseus. "Help me to sharpen this log to a point. Quickly. The wine won't keep our friend asleep for much longer." With knives and flints they shaped the end of the log to a point, and then placed it in the fire until it glowed white hot. Holding the spear up high, they carefully climbed the mountainous stomach of the Cyclops, pointing the spear at the eye....

The screams of the Cyclops echoed around the cave like a roaring tidal wave while, outside, rocks tumbled down the cliff into the sea far below.

Outside, the night sky turned pale but only the bleating of his sheep told the Cyclops that it was morning. Never again would he see daylight. He rolled aside the boulder which blocked the entrance and sat in the gap with his hands spread so that the Greeks couldn't escape. As his sheep pushed forward to get outside, he felt along their sides and backs.

"Those villains aren't going to escape by clinging to your fleeces," he grunted. Little did he realise that Odysseus had roped the sheep together in threes and, under each middle sheep, a man clung for his life.

So Odysseus and his men escaped and ran quickly back to the safety of their ships. Once there, Odysseus called back, "It was I, Odysseus, who blinded you, Polyphemus."

The Cyclops picked up a boulder and hurled it towards the ships, calling, "I am Polyphemus, son of Poseidon the sea god. I will call on my father to destroy you."

Deep in the ocean, Poseidon heard what had happened and, in his anger, sent storms to drive Odysseus further from his home.

Note: this section contains facsimile of OHTs/posters which do not also appear as copymasters.

17

The _____ Revenge

Hear me, _____,
_____,
great god of the _____!
Send me _____, send me _____,
send me _____,
send me _____ too
for the skies to contain!
May _____ with your _____,
close round Odysseus
and his fine men;
may they _____
may they _____;
may they never set foot
on their own lands
again!

© Cambridge University Press 2001

Judith Nicholls, 'The Cyclops' Revenge'

16

The Cyclops' Revenge

Hear me, Poseidon,
hail-thrower, wave-maker,
brewer of foam and flood,
great god of the sea!
Send me winds, send me rain,
send me hurricane, storm;
send me tempests too black
for the skies to contain!
May Charybdis' wild waters
hiss with your fury,
close round Odysseus
and his fine men;
may they lurch from their ships
may they sink to your sands;
may they never set foot
on their own lands
again!

© Cambridge University Press 2001

Judith Nicholls, 'The Cyclops' Revenge'

Note: this section contains facsimile of OHTs/posters which do not also appear as copymasters.

19

The planets

There are nine major planets in Earth's solar system.

All the planets move around the Sun, in elliptical orbits.

There are natural satellites, such as moons, in orbit around some of the planets.

The inner planets

These are closest to the Sun and are known as the terrestrial planets. They are:

- **Mercury:** the closest planet to the Sun.
- **Venus:** the brightest planet in the sky.
- **Earth:** the only planet capable of supporting life.
- **Mars:** the nearest neighbour of Earth.

The outer planets

These are known as the major planets, with the exception of Pluto.

- **Jupiter**
- **Saturn**
- **Uranus**
- **Neptune**
- **Pluto**

Some scientists believe they have detected strong gravitational disturbances at the far edge of the solar system. They suspect that these could be caused by a tenth planet in orbit around the Sun, just beyond Pluto.

Glossary
photosphere: the outermost visible layer of the Sun
X-rays: rays that can pass through many substances that light cannot penetrate

Sources
Encarta (1999)
The Hutchinson Encyclopedia (1998)
Exploring the Planets by Iain Nicolson

18

THE SOLAR SYSTEM

A 'solar system' is the name for a star (or Sun) and all the bodies orbiting it: the planets, their moons, the asteroids and the comets. The planets are held in orbit by the gravitational pull of the star. Each planet spins on its own axis, creating its own gravitational force.

Earth's solar system may be one of millions in the universe. It is thought to have been formed about 4.6 billion years ago. It consists of nine planets, of which the Earth is one, in orbit around a central Sun.

The Sun

The Sun is a star of medium brightness and average size. Once a month, it rotates on its axis. Its dazzling *photosphere* is speckled with bright patches and dark sunspots. The Sun provides daylight and heat. It is a massive ball of burning gases. Within its hot, dense interior, hydrogen atoms are fused together to form helium. As a result, four million tons of the Sun's matter is changed into energy every second. As well as light and heat, the Sun radiates other types of energy, including *X-rays* and radio waves.

Note: this section contains facsimile of OHTs/posters which do not also appear as copymasters.

Non-chronological reports

Mars

Mars is the nearest neighbour of Earth. The surface of Mars is often hidden by storm clouds of yellow dust. Its rocky mountains are orange and red due to iron 'rust' in weathered surfaces. It is, therefore, sometimes called the 'red planet'. On its dusty surface there are old, dry canals visible, showing that there may once have been water on the planet. Now, however, it is dry and cold on Mars. It has a thin atmosphere of carbon dioxide and polar ice-caps of solid carbon dioxide, known as 'dry ice'. Mars has two moons, called Phobus and Deimos.

Personal notes

M = E's nrst n'br; surf. hidden yellow storm clds; orange red mtns. – iron rust ∴ red pl. Canals ∴ prob. once water – now cold + dry. Atmos = dry ice poles (CO₂). 2 moons = Phobus & Deimos.

Non-chronological reports

Earth is the third planet from the sun and the fifth largest of the lot. It is definitely the best planet in the solar system – it's the only one capable of supporting intelligent life forms (like me!). And, of course, this is mainly because of one important thing! Many different life forms can exist on Earth because of its abundant water! There are oceans and seas and rivers and puddles. From space, the planet appears kind of blue because of its water, resulting in Earth's alternative title, the 'blue planet'.

There are lots of different climates around the globe. But it's a pity we don't get more hot days in summer! There are areas of extreme heat, extreme cold and sort of average weather. I think it's pretty obvious from that why we get such different kinds of flora and fauna in different countries. Earth's lovely rich atmosphere is full of oxygen for all the life forms to breathe.

On top of all that, Earth has its very own satellite, the Moon. The Moon's gravitational pull is the thing that makes tidal currents in the oceans. At night the Moon lights up Earth's skies by reflecting the light of the Sun. However, the Moon is also responsible for werewolves and madness.

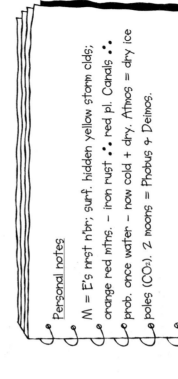

Note: this section contains facsimile of OHTs/posters which do not also appear as copymasters.

24

Isabel met a troublesome doctor,
He pinched and he poked till he really shocked her.
The doctor's talk was of coughs and chills
And the doctor's satchel bulged with pills.
The doctor said unto Isabel,
Swallow this, it will make you well.
Isabel, Isabel didn't worry,
Isabel didn't scream or scurry,
She took those pills from the pill concoctor,
And Isabel calmly cured the doctor.

Isabel once was asleep in bed
When a horrible dream crawled into her head.
It was worse than a dinosaur, worse than a shark,
Worse than an octopus oozing in the dark.
Boo! said the dream, with a dreadful grin,
I'm going to scare you out of your skin!
Isabel, Isabel didn't worry,
Isabel didn't scream or scurry,
Isabel had a cleverer scheme;
She just woke up and fooled that dream.
Remember when you meet a bugaboo
Remember what Isabel used to do.
Don't scream when the bugaboo says Boo!
Just look it in the eye and say Boo to you!
That's how to banish a bugaboo;
Isabel did it and so can you!
Boooooo to you.

Ogden Nash, 'The Adventures of Isabel'

23

The Adventures of Isabel

Isabel met an enormous bear,
Isabel, Isabel didn't care.
The bear was hungry, the bear was ravenous,
The bear's big mouth was cruel and cavernous.
The bear said, Isabel, glad to meet you,
How do, Isabel, now I'll eat you!
Isabel, Isabel didn't worry,
Isabel didn't scream or scurry,
She washed her hands and she straightened her hair up,
Then Isabel quietly ate the bear up.

Once in a night as black as pitch
Isabel met a wicked witch.
The witch's face was cross and wrinkled,
The witch's gums with teeth were sprinkled.
Ho ho, Isabel! the old witch crowed,
I'll turn you into an ugly toad!
Isabel, Isabel didn't worry,
Isabel didn't scream or scurry,
She showed no rage, she showed no rancour,
But she turned the witch into milk and drank her!

Isabel met a hideous giant,
Isabel continued self-reliant.
The giant was hairy, the giant was horrid,
He had one eye in the middle
   of his forehead.
Good morning, Isabel, the giant said,
I'll grind your bones to make my bread.
Isabel, Isabel didn't worry,
Isabel didn't scream or scurry,
She nibbled the zwieback that she always fed off,
And when it was gone, she cut the giant's head off.

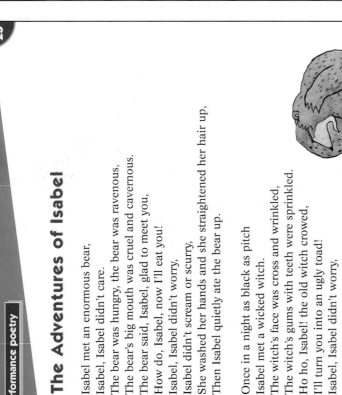

Ogden Nash, 'The Adventures of Isabel'

Note: this section contains facsimile of OHTs/posters which do not also appear as copymasters.

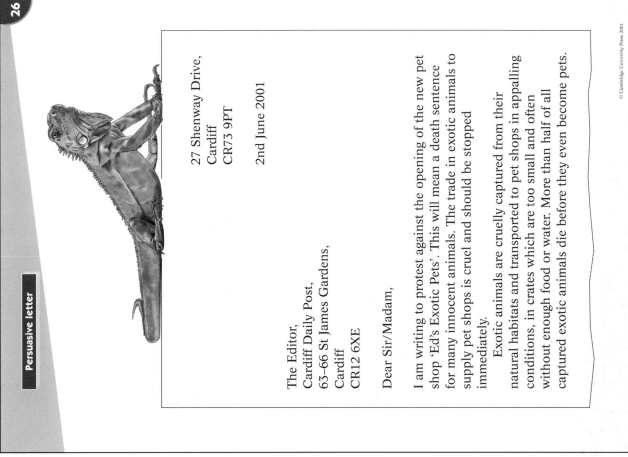

26

Persuasive letter

27 Shenway Drive,
Cardiff
CR73 9PT

2nd June 2001

The Editor,
Cardiff Daily Post,
63–66 St James Gardens,
Cardiff
CR12 6XE

Dear Sir/Madam,

I am writing to protest against the opening of the new pet shop 'Ed's Exotic Pets'. This will mean a death sentence for many innocent animals. The trade in exotic animals to supply pet shops is cruel and should be stopped immediately.

Exotic animals are cruelly captured from their natural habitats and transported to pet shops in appalling conditions, in crates which are too small and often without enough food or water. More than half of all captured exotic animals die before they even become pets.

© Cambridge University Press 2001

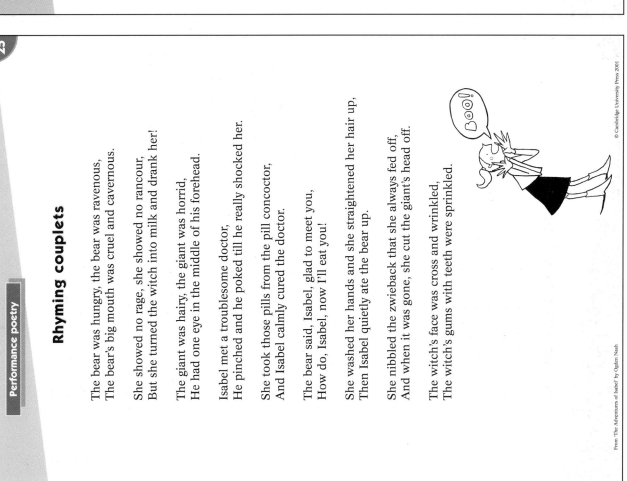

25

Performance poetry

Rhyming couplets

The bear was hungry, the bear was ravenous,
The bear's big mouth was cruel and cavernous.

She showed no rage, she showed no rancour,
But she turned the witch into milk and drank her!

The giant was hairy, the giant was horrid,
He had one eye in the middle of his forehead.

Isabel met a troublesome doctor,
He pinched and he poked till he really shocked her.

She took those pills from the pill concoctor,
And Isabel calmly cured the doctor.

The bear said, Isabel, glad to meet you,
How do, Isabel, now I'll eat you!

She washed her hands and she straightened her hair up,
Then Isabel quietly ate the bear up.

She nibbled the zwieback that she always fed off,
And when it was gone, she cut the giant's head off.

The witch's face was cross and wrinkled,
The witch's gums with teeth were sprinkled.

From 'The Adventures of Isabel' by Ogden Nash

© Cambridge University Press 2001

Note: this section contains facsimile of OHTs/posters which do not also appear as copymasters.

Facts about the exotic pet trade

- Many exotic animals are captured in their natural habitat.
- Animals are transported in crates according to existing regulations and food and water is provided.
- 51% of captured exotic animals die before they become pets.
- Between October 1998 and 1999, 68 pet shop owners and staff were convicted of cruelty compared to 26 the previous year. 126 people were convicted of neglect and cruelty compared to 58 the previous year.
- Pet shop owners and staff do not require any qualifications to look after exotic animals.
- There are no statistics about how many animals are well cared for as pets.
- Environmental Health Officers inspect pet shops every year.
- Pet shop owners have to apply for licences.
- The RSPCA has found: a starving lizard and a wounded python in pet shops, animals abandoned on the streets.

Furthermore, at the pet shop they are kept in unsuitable, cramped conditions by untrained staff. The number of pet shop owners and staff convicted of cruelty more than doubled between 1998 and 1999. The RSPCA recently found a lizard starving to death in a pet shop and a royal python covered with wounds. Surely this should not be allowed to happen?

Naturally, some owners are capable of looking after exotic animals. However, many are ignorant of their pet's special needs and the fact that many vets will not handle exotic species. Consequently, when their pet becomes ill or too difficult to keep, they simply turn it out to die. The RSPCA have found iguanas, bearded dragons and Burmese pythons abandoned in the street. If this happens, what is to become of these animals?

Therefore, this shop should not be allowed to open and everything possible should be done to stop the exotic animal trade immediately. I urge your readers to sign the petition outside 'Ed's Exotic Pets' and to boycott all shops which already supply exotic pets.

Yours faithfully,

Melanie Cooper

(Mrs M. Cooper)

Note: this section contains facsimile of OHTs/posters which do not also appear as copymasters.

Persuasive letter

30

RSPCA calls for check on sale of exotic pets

- The RSPCA is calling on local councils to tighten their checks on the sale of exotic pets. It follows a string of cruelty cases involving pet shops, and an upsurge in cases of exotic animals found abandoned and starving, as ITN's Tim Wilcox reports.

- Between October 1998 and October 1999, the animal welfare organisation secured 68 convictions against pet shop owners and staff compared with 26 the previous year. In one case a lizard was found starving to death in a Leeds pet shop and a royal python was discovered covered in wounds in a Sunderland shop.

- During the same period, neglect and cruelty convictions involving exotic animals rose from 58 to 126. Unwanted animals found in the streets around the country included Burmese pythons, a snapping turtle, iguanas and bearded dragons.

- The RSPCA wants local authorities to toughen its pet shop licences by insisting on a range of measures including an annual veterinary inspection for each shop and a ban on one day licences for 'pet fairs'.

- The society also wants written welfare information to be provided for all animals sold.

From www.itn.co.uk

© Cambridge University Press 2001

Persuasive letter

29

Circus animals: information

- Visitors to circuses can see animals that they would never normally see.

- People learn a lot about animals by visiting circuses.

- Animals are ill-treated in circuses.

- Trained keepers and vets look after the circus animals.

- Animals die prematurely in circuses.

- Circus animals can show abnormal behaviour such as pacing, and chewing the bars of their cages.

- Animals that are not needed are destroyed, sold or abandoned.

- The animals are kept in spacious, clean enclosures.

- Some animals are taken from the wild to perform in circuses.

- Circuses give money to establish conservation centres for endangered animals.

© Cambridge University Press 2001

Note: this section contains facsimile of OHTs/posters which do not also appear as copymasters.

32

Persuasive letter

PETS WILL PERISH IN NEW SHOP!

STOP ED'S EXOTIC PETS BEFORE IT'S TOO LATE!

IS THIS WHAT YOU REALLY WANT TO SEE IN ROSSINGTON?

Ed's Exotic Pets

Did you know that...?

- Animals are cruelly captured in the wild to supply this shop.
- These exotic animals should be living in their natural habitat.
- Half of the captured animals will die before they reach Rossington.
- Animals will be kept in cramped spaces.
- There are no properly trained staff to care for the animals.
- Animals will not be properly fed in the shop.
- Owners will 'dump' unwanted pets in our town.

Sign the petition and
STOP IT NOW!

31

Persuasive letter

BRITISH COLUMBIA SOCIETY FOR THE PREVENTION OF CRUELTY TO ANIMALS

Removing wild animals from their natural habitat can have the following consequences:

- Fragile ecosystems are disturbed as people invade the natural environment to collect wild creatures.

- Capturing wild animals can threaten the species' existence. This is the case with endangered tarantula varieties (Mexican red-legged, Chilean rose, Asian black velvet) – all because of the pet trade.

- More than half of all captured animals die before becoming pets. Their deaths involve great suffering and the surviving animals face cruel treatment, unsuitable living conditions and inadequate diets.

- Many pet owners who grow tired of their exotic pets mistakenly think that releasing them is a humane option. In reality, this creates two possible problems:

  the freed animals die in an inhospitable environment,

  or...

  they thrive, multiply and create a new problem by upsetting the local ecosystem.

Term one fiction focus:
1 How to write a playscript

What most children will already know:	**What children will learn in this unit:**
The basic conventions of play writing	How to develop setting and characterisation in a play
How to read and perform playscripts	How to write production notes
How a story-line is shown in a play	How to divide a play into scenes
How to write a playscript using a known story as a basis	How to write their own play using plot and scene plans
To identify adverbs and understand that they are used to qualify verbs	How to use dramatic techniques in performance
	How to evaluate a script and performance

1 How a play is organised

Objectives

To revise the structure of a play

To investigate the use of stage directions, and pace

To understand that a first scene contains information on character, setting and problem

Shared session

You need: OHT/poster 1, 3 different colour OHT pens, large sheet of paper for class poster.

It is recommended that children have lots of experience of reading and performing published plays before tackling this unit. It will also be useful for children to have covered work on adverbs (Word level 10) and to have a class word bank of adverbs to use when writing their own plays.

- Tell children they are going to learn how to write, perform and review their own play.

- Recap the differences between plays and stories (e.g. plays contain dialogue without speech marks; they have scenes, not chapters; the plot is revealed by characters' actions and dialogue).

- Discuss the **purpose** of plays (e.g. to entertain and/or inform). Explain that this is also the purpose of stories, but plays are written to be acted and **performed**, whereas stories are read – sometimes to an audience, but often for personal pleasure.

- Look at OHT/poster 1. Explain that this playscript has been adapted from the beginning of a story by Anne Fine (*Crummy Mummy and Me*). Ask children to think what the story is about, as you read it. Now read the playscript and discuss responses.

- Ask how we know whose turn it is to speak in this first scene. Underline the characters' names.

- Ask if the playwright gives us any help with how to read the dialogue (e.g. question marks and exclamation marks). Identify and mark these on the text. Identify the **ellipsis** (…). Ask what effect this has on how we read the script (e.g. it builds up tension by creating a pause).

- Now ask children to identify the **stage directions** relating to voice (*shouting angrily, calling, sighing, cheerfully*). Revise the term **adverb**. Underline these words in a different colour and write *stage directions* on the script.

- Split the class into two groups, Mum and Minna. Read the dialogue aloud, using appropriate expression.

- Ask what other help stage directions can give to actors (e.g. ideas about movements and actions on the stage). Use a different colour to underline the stage directions relating to action.

- Discuss the **pace** of the scene. Will it all be acted at the same speed, or will some lines be delivered faster than others? What is the dramatic effect of this? For example, lines up to *You'll freeze* could be acted at a fast pace, to emphasise Minna's tension about being late. The next two lines could be spoken more slowly, to emphasise the emotion here, before the pace picks up for the last line.

You may wish to take one of these parts yourself at first to demonstrate, especially if the class lacks confidence in drama.

- Ask two volunteers to act out the scene, following all the stage directions, and thinking about the pace.

- Revise the information that usually goes at the beginning of stories (characters, setting, problem). Is the same information given at the beginning of this play? Identify the characters (Minna and Mum), the setting (home) and the problem (Minna has an unusual Mum and she is late for school).

- Tell children they are going to investigate another scene from this play.

Group follow-up activities

 1 red pupil's book page 4 copymaster 1

Children read the given scene. They identify different elements in the script, underlining them in different colours. They then rehearse and perform the scene.

Guided group support Recap the functions of the different elements of the playscript. Help children consider the stage directions in their performance.

 2 blue pupil's book page 4 copymaster 2

Children read the given scene. They add stage directions relating to speech and movement, using the word bank in the pupil's book. They then rehearse and perform the scene.

Guided group support Focus on using suitable stage directions. Ask children to explain their choice. Discuss how the needs of the audience can be reflected in the performance of this scene.

 3 yellow pupil's book page 5

Children read the given narrative. They write it as a scene for a play, including stage directions. They then rehearse the scene, taking into account the pace of different sections, and perform it.

Guided group support As with the blue group. Focus also on the pace of different sections, and how this can be reflected in the performance.

Alternative group activity

 red/blue/yellow pupil's book pages 6–7

Children read a narrative. They write it as a play, including stage directions. They can use the word bank on page 4 of the pupil's book to help.

Plenary

It doesn't matter if all the children do not perform at this stage – the process of rehearsing and the discussion it generates is more important.

Ask children what they have learnt about writing plays from this session. Make a poster to write up their responses. Call it 'How to write a brilliant play'.
Ask volunteers to perform the scenes they have been working on. Give the audience a 'listening target' related to the group's objectives (e.g. is the scene paced well? What do you think is the speech stage direction for that particular line?).

2 How to create characters in a play

Objectives To develop characterisation through dialogue and action

To explore similarities and differences in presenting characters in stories and plays

Shared session *You need: OHTs/posters 1, 2 and 3, class poster (from Session 1).*

- Tell children you are going to find out how to create characters for your play.

- First, you are going to find out what kind of person Mum is by looking at Scene 1 of the playscript on OHT/poster 1. Split the class into two groups and re-read this.

Character profile
Name: 'Mum'
Appearance: punk
Age: about 30
Personality: untidy, caring, sensitive, unconventional, disorganised

- Use a large piece of paper to draw up a character profile of Mum (see margin). Ask children what information we have about Mum (she has two children – Minna, who goes to school, and a baby). Use the picture on OHT/poster 1 to write about Mum's appearance.

- Ask the children what kind of person they think Mum is, and how they know. Discuss that we do not have a direct description of character, as we might in a narrative. We have to look at dialogue, stage directions (for speech and action), and how other characters react to them. Children might suggest that Mum is:
  - untidy (she never puts her shoes away);
  - sensitive (she feels sad that she embarrasses Minna);
  - a good mother (Minna hugs her and tells her she isn't a *Crummy Mummy*).

- Point out that, although we know a lot about Mum from Scene 1, there are still many things we don't know – for example, are there more people in the family? Is there something else about her personality which we don't know yet? How will she react to different people? This information may be revealed in later scenes.

- Tell children that when they write their own plays they do not have to reveal everything about their characters in the first scene. Their characters can develop during the play, and may surprise us, even in the last scene!

- Explain that you are going to meet a new character in the story: Mum's boyfriend, Crusher Maggot. Read OHT/poster 2.

- Note that this is narrative and not a play, therefore we are being told what Crusher is like by the story-teller. As the story is in the first person, the story-teller is Minna.

- Tell children you are going to write some dialogue for Crusher. Emphasise that this must reflect Crusher's personality. You need to decide what he says, how he says it, and what his actions are.

- Work together on OHT/poster 3. Write the stage directions and the dialogue in two different colours.

- When you have finished, split the class into two groups and read your new scene. Discuss how effective the dialogue and stage directions are in giving a good picture of Crusher Maggot.

Group follow-up activities **1 red   pupil's book page 8**

This activity will also work well using a book the children have read, possibly in guided reading.

Children read character profiles based on characters from *Crummy Mummy and Me*. They read lines of dialogue and decide who said each one, giving a reason for their choice.

Guided group support Focus on how each line of dialogue reflects a character's personality.

2 blue   pupil's book page 9   copymaster 3

Children write a character profile for Crusher and then insert his dialogue and stage directions into a given scene.

Guided group support Help children reflect a character's personality through dialogue and stage directions.

3 yellow   pupil's book page 9

Children read the narrative about Gran and write a character profile.

4 yellow   pupil's book page 9

Children act out a scene between Gran and Mum. They then write it as a play.

Guided group support As with the blue group. Help children make their dialogue more effective by using metaphors and similes.

Alternative group activities   **red/blue   pupil's book page 10**

Children look at a picture and two character profiles in the pupil's book. They work with a partner to improvise a conversation between the two characters and then script the scene.

yellow   pupil's book page 11

Children choose one of the characters pictured, ensuring it is different from the one chosen by their partner. They write a character profile and choose a suggested scene to act out with their partner's character. They then script the scene.

Plenary   Return to your class poster from Session 1. Write the sub-heading 'Characters', and ask children what they have learnt about writing characters in a play. Recap that in plays characters' personalities are shown through dialogue, action and other characters' reactions.

Ask children to read out scenes from their activities, while the others listen carefully to the dialogue and try to assess the characters' personalities. After the scene has been read, ask children what they know about these characters and how they have found out this information.

3 How to create settings in a play

Objectives   To learn how to set a scene in a play, using production notes

To understand the effectiveness of sound and lighting in emphasising key features in a scene

Shared session   *You need: OHT/poster 1, class poster (from Session 2).*

■ Tell children they are going to learn how to create settings in a play.

■ Return to OHT/poster 1. Ask where the scene is set (in the hallway of the house). Discuss what we know about the hallway from the playscript (e.g. it has stairs, because the stage directions tell us that *Minna stands at the bottom of the stairs* and Mum comes *running downstairs*).

- Explain that plays often contain **production notes**, which give the people who are putting on the play more information about the setting. Tell children you are going to write some production notes for this scene.

- Ask what information these production notes might contain. First of all, consider the props and scenery – explain that this is called the **set**. Ask for suggestions. What does the hall <u>look like</u>? Is the house tidy or messy? What might be lying about the hall? Think about what Mum is looking for. Think about the weather outside. Is there any way to show this? Write these ideas up on the board/flipchart (see below for examples).

- Emphasise that production notes are written in the present tense, and must give clear information to set designers and the people who organise the props.

- Ask what additional information production notes could have. Discuss the importance of **sound** in creating an atmosphere. Again, ask for suggestions (see below for examples). You might want to consider how certain sounds, such as music, could emphasise particular characters.

- Discuss how **lighting** too can create atmosphere. Explain that lighting should focus the audience's attention on the most important character at a particular moment. Help children see how this focus changes in this scene, and ask how the lighting could change to show this. Suggest that a spotlight might be useful here.

- Your production notes may look like this:

  Set: The house is untidy, with a pile of Mum's shoes at the bottom of the stairs. There is a window by the front door, and snow is falling.

  Lighting: The spotlight starts on Minna and switches to Mum, following her down the stairs.

  Sound: There is a radio on in the background playing punk music.

- Tell children they are going to write production notes for other scenes in the play.

Group follow-up activities

1 red   pupil's book page 12

Children use a picture of the set for the kitchen. They write production notes for the scene.

Guided group support Focus on writing production notes in the present tense.

2 blue   pupil's book page 13

Children read a description of another scene from *Crummy Mummy and Me,* and write production notes for it. If there is time they could then draw the set.

Guided group support Discuss what the garden will look like – how will children show the difference between the two halves? What else needs to be in the scene? (an old car) Help children think of ideas for sound and lighting.

3 yellow   pupil's book page 13

Children read an extract from *Crummy Mummy and Me*. They write production notes for the scene described. If there is time they could then draw the set.

Guided group support Focus on writing production notes which take account of all the elements needed in the scene. Discuss how to use sound and lighting effects to emphasise key points in the text.

Plenary Return to your class poster from Session 2. Write another sub-heading 'Settings'. Ask children what they have learnt about how to show settings in their play. Write their comments on the poster. Emphasise the need to write production notes about set, sound and lighting.

Ask children to explain their own production notes to the rest of the class, explaining why they have chosen certain objects, sound and lighting effects.

Planning the plot for a play

Objectives
To plan a strong plot for the play

To understand how a play is divided into scenes

Shared session   *You need: OHT/poster 4, a large sheet of paper, class poster (from Session 3).*

It is possible to jump straight to Session 5, and plan the play from the stimulus on the planning sheets without using the storyboard. However, this session allows children to focus exclusively on plot, leaving character and setting for later. It is especially effective with middle and lower ability children whose plot often gets 'lost' in the middle section of a story or play.

■ Tell children they are going to plan a **plot** for their play. Establish an audience for this play.

■ Emphasise that the plot is just as important in a play as in a story, and follows the same structure. Revise this structure (a problem in the beginning, events leading to a climax/conflict in the middle, and a resolution at the end).

■ With the children, establish the story-line for your play, using the most appropriate stimulus for your class. Here are some ideas:

   ● Use the characters from *Crummy Mummy and Me* and write a play about another incident in their lives – for example, going on holiday.

   ● Use another curriculum area, such as history. A Victorian focus could be a story based on the life of a working child; a Greek focus might be the siege of Troy. (N.B. Historical artefacts can provide good stimuli for playwriting.)

   ● Use a story that children have already written, and turn it into a playscript.

   ● Use a character/characters from a novel you have studied, and write a sequel as a playscript.

■ Discuss the plot of your chosen story.

■ Now use OHT/poster 4 to write notes for the plot, using the same conventions as for planning a story. Plan the beginning and the problem first, then the end, and finally the middle. Five scenes will create a balanced play.

■ Ask children when they think it is appropriate to have a change of scene. Discuss what new elements might be introduced in new scenes (e.g. a change of setting; new characters; a change of characters; a different event). Explain or revise that each scene has an introduction, main event and a conclusion.

■ Alternatively, you may wish to plan using a **storyboard**, to show the main focus of each scene. If so, draw the main action for each scene – stick people are fine!

Group follow-up activities

1 It is very important that children work together on this, as they will need to write and perform their plays co-operatively.
2 The number of scenes may be increased or decreased according to the confidence of each group. You may wish to white-out some of the sections on copymaster 4, or use new sheets of A3 paper.

1 red/blue   pupil's book page 14   copymaster 4

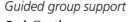

Children use pictures to help them plan a plot for their play. Alternatively, they can use ideas they have come up with in the shared session.

Guided group support

Red On the copymaster, write in the plot notes for the beginning and end so that children complete only the middle section. Alternatively, draw a complete storyboard and ask children to write the plot notes from this.

Blue Help children include three scenes in the middle of the play that build to a conflict/climax.

2 yellow   pupil's book page 15   copymaster 4

Children use a postcard to help them plan a plot for their play. Alternatively, they can use their own ideas from the shared session.

Guided group support Help children include four or five main events in the middle section of the play. Encourage them to introduce more complex plot-lines.

Plenary Return to your class poster from Session 3. Discuss what children have learnt about the importance of planning a strong plot for a play, and how a play is split into scenes. Add this to the poster.

(5) Planning scenes, settings and characters

Objectives To plan settings and action for each scene of the play

To plan characters for the play

Shared session *You need: OHT/poster 4 (saved from Session 4), a large sheet of paper for poster, copymaster 5 (enlarged to A3), class poster (from Session 4).*

■ Tell children they are going to make detailed plans for their plays.

■ Display your class plan on OHT/poster 4. Remind children that this gives us details of the plot, but there is other information we need to know before drafting. Elicit/prompt what this information is:

   ○ where each scene is set;

   ○ the personalities of the characters;

   ○ which characters are in each scene.

■ Begin by planning the characters. Ask children what we call a list of characters in a play (the **cast**). Recap on the cast for your play.

[picture of the character]
Name: _____
Age: _____
Appearance: _____
_____
Personality: _____
_____
_____

■ Make a poster to use for character profiles. Include no more than four main characters – any more will be difficult for children to handle. It is not necessary to write profiles for minor characters. Draw up each profile as shown in the margin.

■ Draw a sketch of what each character looks like, and fill in the character profile in note form. Refer back to the character profiles in Session 2 if necessary. Remind children that characters' personalities will be revealed mainly through action and dialogue in the play.

■ Use an enlarged version of copymaster 5 to plan each scene. Complete the 'Action' section first. Use your storyboard pictures and notes, but ask for more detail. Point out that the plot is still in the planning stage, and can be changed if anyone has better ideas.

■ Write notes about the setting for each scene. Do not include too much detail here: this will be provided by the production notes for each scene.

■ Finally, plan which characters are going to be involved in each scene.

Group follow-up activities **red/blue/yellow   pupil's book page 16   copymaster 5**

As in Session 4, you may wish to white-out scene sections on copymaster 5 or provide extra copies, for children writing fewer or more scenes in their plays.

Children plan their plays in pairs or groups. They write character profiles and then fill in the scene plan on copymaster 5.

Guided group support

Red Fill in the 'Action' sections on copymaster 5 yourself. Ask children to complete details of the setting and the characters for each scene.

Blue Focus on providing details about the characters.

Yellow Focus on producing detailed character profiles.

Plenary   Return to your class poster from Session 4. Write a sub-heading, 'Planning', and ask children what they have learnt about planning a play. Refer to scenes, characters and settings. Ask about any difficulties which occurred when completing the plan and how these were overcome. Ask children to share their play plans. Discuss characters, setting and action.

6 Drafting the play

Objectives   To write play scenes, using the correct page layout

To include information about the characters' personalities in the dialogue

To write appropriate production notes and stage directions

Shared session   *You need: character profiles poster, scene plan (multiple copies), character labels (see below), class poster (from Session 5).*

*1 See **Drafting** on page 7 for more detailed advice on conducting a whole-class drafting session.*
You will need to spread this stage over several lessons, drafting one or two scenes each time. For example, you could draft the first scene in one lesson, the middle two or three scenes in another lesson and the last scene in a third.

2 Mixed ability groups work well for this activity.

■ Tell children they are going to use their plans to draft the scenes in their plays.

■ For each scene you tackle, look at your scene plan. Note the setting, action and the characters who are going to be involved. Re-read the character profiles to remind children about the personalities of the characters involved in the scene.

■ Next, split the class into groups, each containing the number of characters in the scene. Explain they are going to create dialogue for this scene.

■ Decide who is going to play each character. Use sticky labels with the names of the characters written on, and distribute them. This helps children get 'in character'.

■ Appoint a 'director' for each group. Their responsibility is to oversee the scene, making sure that the plot is clear, and that the audience understand who the characters are, and something about them. The director will also have the power to cut lines, or to give suggestions for dialogue. Give the director a copy of the shared scene plan.

■ Children then improvise dialogue and actions. Set a time limit for this, say five or ten minutes. If groups are struggling, provide cards with suggestions for the first few lines of dialogue already written out.

■ Now ask groups to perform their scenes. Ask the others to consider critically the dialogue and actions. After performance, ask which group made the plot clear, and most accurately portrayed the characters. How did they achieve this?

■ Now demonstrate how to script the scene. Talk through each stage of writing as you work. Show how a play is set out (speakers' names separately on the left; stage directions in brackets; no speech marks).

■ Ask children for ideas for dialogue and action from their improvisations. Take lines from various groups, pulling together the strongest portrayal of characters.

■ Experiment with different stage directions. What effect is given if the direction is *shouted loudly*, rather than *whispered menacingly*? Which gives a more accurate portrayal of the character?

■ Next, write the production notes for the scene. Refer back to the notes you made on the class poster in Session 3.

- Finally, ask for volunteers to perform the scene. Ask the others to listen carefully to the delivery of lines, and the use of stage directions. Discuss whether the scene is successful in showing the plot and personalities of the characters.

Group follow-up activities

Children will need stickers on which to write their characters' names. One child may have to take more than one part.

red/blue/yellow

As in the shared session, children use their play plans to improvise scenes and then draft them.

Guided group support

Red Focus on writing dialogue which clearly shows the plot. The writing of production notes is optional for this group – you may wish to provide these yourself.

Blue Focus on showing characterisation through dialogue and action. Help children include simple production notes.

Yellow As with the blue group. Encourage children to produce clear production notes that show the use of sound and lighting for dramatic effect.

Plenary

Ask groups to perform scenes. Afterwards, discuss which group brought out the plot most clearly, and most accurately portrayed the characters. How did they do this? Draw out some teaching points from this discussion – for example:

- make sure that the dialogue is either moving the plot on, or telling us something about the character;
- make sure that actions are relevant to the plot or to the characters – it's OK to stand still!

Add these points to your class poster as 'Top Tips for Playwrights'. Use these tips in subsequent drafting lessons and add further ideas as you go along.

7 Revising and editing the play

Objectives

To assess the effectiveness of the script

To improve the script by redrafting

Shared session

You need: draft playscript (multiple copies).

*1 See **Revising and editing** on page 7 for more detailed advice.*

2 Revising a playscript uses essentially the same techniques as revising a story. However, the measure of a playscript's success is how effective it is in performance. Therefore, in order to revise the playscript, children will need to <u>rehearse</u> changes to the dialogue and action.

- Tell children they are going to revise their playscripts.
- Choose a revision focus. It may be something that children have had difficulties with in their drafting – for example:
  - **characterisation** – look at the original character profile. Do the characters' actions and dialogue reflect their personality? Is there any dialogue or action that could be changed to provide a more accurate portrayal?
  - **plot** – is the plot clear? Do the audience understand what is happening? How could this be improved?
  - **stage directions** – are they used effectively? Could they be improved through clearer language?
  - **production notes** – are they clear? Have sound and lighting been used to good effect? How could this be improved?

- Hand out copies of the shared playscript for children to work on. Write the revision focus at the top of the script, then ask volunteers to perform scenes. Ask those listening to think how the focus can be improved.

- Work together to improve the playscript. Ask children to modify their copies of the playscript as well, then perform the revised version.

- Assess the revised playscript for effectiveness.

Group follow-up activities

You may wish to correct other errors which are not part of the revision focus, or spend another session proofreading the scripts for spelling and punctuation errors.

red/blue/yellow

Children revise their playscripts. Identify a revision focus for each group.

Guided group support

Red Ensure that the dialogue makes sense, and that the plot is clear.

Blue Help improve characterisation by looking at dialogue and action.

Yellow As with the blue group. Consider the use of sound and lighting to enhance dramatic effect.

Plenary Children feed back on their revising and editing work. They report on what they have learnt, and how this will help them improve their scriptwriting in the future. Ask children for examples of something in their script which they have changed, and how this change has improved their play.

8 Publishing the play

Objectives To understand the differences between publishing a story and a play

To publish a completed play

Shared session *You need: a selection of published plays and stories.*

1 See Publishing on page 8 for more detailed notes on the issues involved in the final presentation of the text.

2 Here are some good examples of plays published specifically for use in schools:
Fantastic Mr Fox, adapted by Sally Reid;
James and the Giant Peach, adapted by Richard R. George;
Bill's New Frock, adapted by Anne Fine.
These plays are all adapted from narratives. Use them to compare the layout of the playscript with the original narrative.

- Hand out a selection of plays and stories (see margin for suggestions). Children work in groups on a large piece of paper. Ask them to draw up a list of similarities and differences between publishing a play and a story – for example:

  Similarities
  - ⊙ eye-catching front covers and blurbs
  - ⊙ author and illustrators' names on the front of the book

  Differences
  - ⊙ playscripts have fewer illustrations (not as important as in stories)
  - ⊙ stories are often split into chapters; playscripts are split into scenes
  - ⊙ playscripts begin with a cast of characters
  - ⊙ the dialogue and stage directions in playscripts are often in different fonts; narrative and speech in stories are in the same font

- Discuss these findings as a class. Use them to draw up some 'Rules for Publishing a Play'. These might include:
  - ⊙ Start with a cast list.
  - ⊙ Characters' names should be written in the margin in capital letters (or bold).
  - ⊙ Stage directions should be written in a different colour (or italics).
  - ⊙ ...and others which will be unique to your class!

Plan the front cover of the class play, and write the blurb together.

Group follow-up activities   **red/blue/yellow**

Children work on publishing their own plays.

Guided group support

Red Ensure that children's plays are split into scenes. Make sure it is clear which character is speaking.

Blue Help children distinguish clearly between dialogue and stage directions.

Yellow As with the blue group.

Plenary   Look at the completed plays. Assess the strengths of each one. Children act out scenes from each other's plays to find out which they think are clear to follow, and why.

9 Performing and evaluating the play

Objectives   To annotate a playscript for performance

To consider audience needs

To perform a play from a script

To evaluate plays critically and give valid reasons for judgements

Shared session   *You need: copies of children's scripts (see below), class playscript, copymaster 6 (multiple copies).*

1 The purpose of writing a playscript is for it to be performed. This should be fulfilled by performing the plays for the chosen audience.

2 You will need to use a large space for this session – for example, the school hall.

■ Make sure you have enough copies of the plays for each group to use for their performance. Groups may need to work together to perform each other's plays as well as their own. Appoint a 'director' to take charge of organising the action, and to consider the needs of the audience.

■ With the children, prepare the necessary props in advance of this session (see the Session 8 homework suggestion).

■ Show children how to annotate their playscripts for performance. Demonstrate this with the shared playscript. For example, when a character is speaking, what can she/he be doing at the same time? What might the other character(s) be doing? (e.g. smiling, frowning, yawning).

■ Revise what children learnt about pace in Session 1. Consider parts of the script which need be delivered at a quicker or slower pace, and annotate this.

■ Children rehearse their plays and perform them for the intended audience.

■ During the performances, children use copymaster 6 to evaluate each other's plays. This can be done in pairs. Organise in advance of the performance who is going to evaluate each play. Demonstrate how to fill in copymaster 6. One evaluation for each play is enough.

■ The results of the evaluation should be shared with the actors and playwrights after the performances. Use this as positive feedback to develop self-confidence and give ideas for improving script writing.

ADDITIONAL SESSIONS

Writing in the style of Anne Fine

Objectives   To investigate the writing style of an author, and how characters are presented

To write a chapter in the style of Anne Fine, using paragraphs to organise writing

Shared session (1)   *You need: OHT/poster 5, a large sheet of paper.*

This Additional session will take two sessions.

■ Tell children they are going to write a new chapter for *Crummy Mummy and Me* in the style of the author, Anne Fine. Establish an audience for your writing.

■ Explain that you need to find out what Anne Fine's style of writing is by looking closely at a section from the book. Together, you are going to make up a set of guidelines on 'How to write like Anne Fine'.

■ Read the extract on OHT/poster 5. Identify and underline key features of Anne Fine's writing in this passage. Make a 'Guidelines' poster. The main points are:

 ○ The story is written in the first person: all events are seen from Minna's viewpoint.
 ○ Minna addresses the reader directly with questions (e.g. *wouldn't you?*).
 ○ Minna comments on situations, often through asides, so that the reader knows how she is feeling (e.g. *I was getting pretty cross.*).
 ○ The style is informal and 'chatty', and uses slang (e.g. *wrapped in a downie*).
 ○ Sarcasm and exaggeration are used (e.g. *purple spots on my belly!*).
 ○ Short sentences are used to emphasise a point (e.g. *I wouldn't. Not any more.*).
 ○ Longer sentences are used to emphasise Minna's chatty style (e.g. *And she said it suspiciously… Pebble Mill at One.*).

■ Ask the children what they know about Minna's character (e.g. she is mature, sensible, funny). Emphasise that we know this because of Minna's dialogue and interaction with characters, and her direct involvement with the reader.

■ Ask children to work in pairs and discuss other phrases that Minna might use, either when speaking directly to another character, or when addressing the reader (e.g. *I couldn't believe it when…*; *Honestly, sometimes I wonder who's the child around here!*).

■ List these on your poster, as a bank of useful phrases for children to use in their own writing.

■ Plan the next part of the chapter together. Revise that each chapter is a mini-story, and should contain a beginning, middle, end, problem, conflict and resolution. Point out that the problem is already established – Minna is ill.

Group follow-up activities (1)   **1 red   pupil's book page 17**

Children copy out a plan with the beginning section already provided. They plan the middle and end of their chapter.

Guided group support Focus on planning connected events in the middle of a story.

2 blue   pupil's book page 17

Children use the given chapter beginning as a stimulus and plan a new chapter.

Guided group support Help children reflect Anne Fine's style in their planning.

3 yellow   pupil's book page 18

Children use chapter headings or a picture as a stimulus and plan a new chapter.

Guided group support As with the blue group.

Plenary (1)   Ask volunteers to read out their story plans. The class listens critically to the plot outlines. Discuss whether they think each one is appropriate for the style of the book.

Shared session (2)   *Display your 'How to write like Anne Fine' poster and the story plan from Shared session 1. Re-read this plan with the class.*

- Write the story chapter with the children. Focus on the style of writing and consistent presentation of character. For example, as you write, ask questions like: would Minna say that? Would she really react in that way?

- Use phrases from the language bank you prepared in Shared session 1. Add others to it as you are writing. This will help children when they write their own chapters.

- Read the completed shared chapter with the class. Ask if it reflects the style of the author and reinforce how this was done.

Group follow-up activities (2)   **red/blue/yellow**

Children draft their chapters.

Guided group support

Red Focus on using paragraphs to structure writing.

Blue Help children write in the specified style, and to use words and phrases specific to each character.

Yellow Focus on maintaining consistency of character and style in children's writing.

Plenary (2)   Ask children to reflect on what they have learnt by using another author's style in their writing. Ask them to share their chapters and listen critically for consistency of style and character.

 Keeping a reading journal

Objective   To record ideas, reflections and predictions about a book in a reading journal

Shared session   *You need: copymaster 7 (enlarged).*

- Display the enlarged version of the reading journal framework on copymaster 7. Discuss using this before, during and after reading. Demonstrate how to use the reading journal with a current shared reading book.

■ Demonstrate completing the prediction section ('I think the book will be about...') with the use of a story map. Ask children for suggestions.

■ Point out that you can build up a profile of a character by drawing the character using descriptions/clues in the book, and labelling the drawing. Alternatively, you can build up a character profile in notes. Explain that you can add to this as you read through the book, and get to know more about the character. Ask for suggestions.

■ Discuss how personal responses (*I liked...*; *I didn't like...*) can be recorded as text, or in pictures.

(N.B. A reading journal should not be a laborious task which has to be completed every time a book is finished. It is suggested that children complete the journal once or twice every half term, using either their guided reading book, or one they are reading for personal pleasure. Less fluent readers may need more structure, and be told when to write comments about a book. For fluent readers, the reading journal may always be on hand to record predictions, responses to events, ongoing thoughts or feelings about characters and interesting vocabulary.)

Group follow-up activities

This is an ongoing task to be completed during independent activities in the Literacy Hour, in silent reading time, as a guided session or at home.

1 red   pupil's book page 19   copymaster 7

Children complete the reading journal framework on the copymaster.

2 blue/yellow   pupil's book page 19

Children create their own reading journal by answering a list of questions about their book.

Writing a poem about feelings

Objectives

To understand how moods and feelings can be presented in poetry

To write a poem which uses words, phrases and metaphors to reflect feelings

Shared session   *You need: OHT/poster 6.*

■ Tell children you are going to read a poem called 'Grandad' by Kit Wright. Ask them to think about the **mood** of the poem as you read it. Read aloud the poem on OHT/poster 6.

■ Discuss the different moods of the poem – the sad tone of the repeated phrase as opposed to the nostalgic, but happier tone of the main verses. Ask how the sad tone is conveyed in the repeated phrase (e.g. it is a short, factual statement that contrasts with the happy memories of Grandad. It is repeated as if the poet has to keep reminding himself that Grandad is dead).

■ Ask children if they can tell from the poem what Grandad was like (e.g. funny, unconventional, caring). Ask them to identify how the poet reveals Grandad's character.

■ Point out the use of exaggeration and metaphor (e.g. *You could have hidden/A football crowd in it.*). Ask for other examples. Discuss how this shows Grandad's character to be 'larger than life'; someone who enjoyed life and was not bound by social rules or expectations.

■ Ask how children think the poet felt about Grandad. Explain that the poet focuses on small details, such as Grandad's coat and hat. These provide an intimacy that a general description would lack. Ask for more examples of these details.

■ Tell children they are going to write a poem to reflect their feelings about someone or something they know or knew well. Establish an audience for these poems.

■ Tell children they are going to think carefully about the person or creature they are writing about, and brainstorm ideas for description. Encourage them to focus on small details, as in 'Grandad', and to use powerful descriptive tools such as metaphor.

■ Discuss the use of a repeated phrase to change the mood of the poem. Can children create one of their own?

Group follow-up activities   **red/blue/yellow**

Children brainstorm ideas for description and then draft their own poems.

Guided group support

Red Help children to organise the layout of their writing as a poem, and to include some descriptive phrases.

Blue Focus on using detailed adjectival phrases. Encourage children to use a repeated phrase to change the mood of the poem.

Yellow As with the blue group. Focus also on using metaphor.

Plenary   Ask children what they have learnt about representing feelings in poetry. Reinforce the focus on detail, the use of specific vocabulary and contrasts within a poem. Ask children to share their work with the rest of the class and to explain how their feelings have been represented in the poem.

Homework suggestions

- Use a book you have at home, or your home reading book. Write a script based on the first scene in the book. **(After Session 1)**

- Create another character for the Anne Fine story, possibly a friend of Crusher's or Mum's. Draw up a character profile, writing information about name, age, appearance and personality. **(After Session 2)**

- Write the production notes for the scene you wrote from your book. **(After Session 3)**

- Draw a storyboard for a cartoon or television programme you know. **(After Session 4)**

- Design a front cover and write a blurb for your play. **(After Session 7)**

- Make a list of props and costumes that you need for your play. Find what you can at home, and bring it to school for the performance. **(After Session 8)**

UNIT **How to write a playscript**

Colour the right number of stars to show how well you did the following things:

0 stars = I didn't do it.   3 stars = I did it well.
1 star = I gave it a try.   4 stars = I did an excellent job!
2 stars = I did it quite well.

I planned a play in scenes.	☆	☆	☆	☆
I wrote a play with a clear layout which was easy to follow.	☆	☆	☆	☆
I wrote clear stage directions.	☆	☆	☆	☆
I set the scene using production notes.	☆	☆	☆	☆
I showed my characters' personalities.	☆	☆	☆	☆
I used my voice expressively in the performance.	☆	☆	☆	☆
I knew what was good about a play and I had suggestions about how to make it better.	☆	☆	☆	☆

Something I am especially pleased with

Something my audience liked in my writing

Something I'd like to do better next time

Term one non-fiction focus:
2 How to write a recount for two different audiences

What most children will already know:

That recounts are usually structured – orientation, events in chronological order, reorientation

That cohesion in recounts is achieved through chronological/temporal connectives

That recounts can be written for a variety of purposes and audiences

That recounts may be personal, journalistic or formal

What children will learn in this unit:

That recounts may be useful in expressing knowledge of a historical period

That some recounts contain personal opinions

To adapt the recount form for a particular purpose and audience

To adapt the language for a particular purpose and audience

---

 1 Looking at a historical recount

Objectives
To investigate the main features of historical recounts

To establish that parts of history books are written in recount form

Shared session
You need: OHT/poster 7.

- Tell children they are going to learn how to plan and write historical recounts for two different audiences.

- Display and read the historical recount on OHT/poster 7. Then use it to revise children's knowledge of recounts. Firstly, ask children what is the purpose of a recount (e.g. to retell and comment on past events).

- Revise the orientation, events and reorientation structure of recounts. Ask children to come up and mark these sections on the OHT/poster. Label each section accordingly (paragraph 1 = orientation; paragraphs 2–4 = events; paragraph 5 = reorientation).

- Ask children what questions the orientation usually answers (*who, what, where, when, why, how*). Ask which of these questions are answered in the first paragraph. Underline the information which answers each question.

- Ask children in which tense recounts are written (past tense). Underline examples on the OHT/poster. Revise the importance of **chronological order** in recounts. Identify and underline examples of **chronological connectives** on the OHT/poster.

- Now consider the detail of the information and the language used in this recount. Ask children if they think it is a formal or informal piece of writing (formal).

- Ask children where they would expect to find this recount (in a history textbook). Consider the evidence for this (the facts are presented clearly and in a serious style, without personal opinion).

■ Now ask children who they think the intended audience is (children of approximately their own age). Again, consider the evidence for this (no assumption is made of expert knowledge).

Group follow-up activities

1 red   pupil's book page 20   copymaster 8

Children look at another historical recount. They identify the orientation, events and reorientation sections and complete a who/what/where/when/why/how grid.

Guided group support Ensure that children are comfortable with the recount form being used in a historical context. Emphasise chronology and past tense presentation.

2 blue   pupil's book page 20

As for activity 1, copying out the grid from the pupil's book.

Guided group support Ensure confidence with the recount form in a historical context, reconciling the notion of 'events in chronological order' with something more like 'past events in sensible order' in the historical context.

3 blue   pupil's book page 21

Children read additional sentences and decide which section they could be added to (orientation, events or reorientation). They then check for sentences which are inappropriate in a formal recount.

4 yellow   pupil's book page 22

As for activity 2, using a more challenging recount.

Guided group support Contrast the formal language in this text with your own spoken language of teaching in the classroom. Talk about why written language in textbooks is often formal – refer to unknown audiences.

5 yellow   pupil's book page 23

As for activity 3, with more challenging sentences.

Plenary

Ask children what they have found out about formal historical recounts from their follow-up activities.

② Adapting a recount for two different audiences

Objective

To identify similarities and differences between formal, personal and journalistic recounts

Shared session

You need: OHTs/posters 8 and 9.

If much of the information here is unfamiliar to children, you may wish to spread this over two lessons.

■ Recap briefly on the historical recount from Session 1. Ask children how you identified that it was a formal recount. Explain that you are going to look at different versions of this original recount, both written for different audiences.

■ Display OHT/poster 8. Ask children where they would expect to see this piece of writing (in a newspaper). Identify and label the headline, photo and caption.

■ Read OHT/poster 8 with the class. Establish that this text is also about the siege of Troy. Recap what is usually in the orientation, events and reorientation sections of recounts. Identify and underline these features in the text.

- Ask children what makes this recount different from the one they looked at in Session 1 (e.g. the layout; it contains only the basic facts; the writing is entertaining and more immediate; it contains direct quotes).

- Ask who the audience for this text would be (children; a 'pretend' readership of a newspaper). Help children see that, while this recount is less formal than the one on OHT/poster 7, it is still written for an unknown audience.

- Now read the letter on OHT/poster 9. Ask children to identify the layout – greeting and closure. As before, recap what is usually in the orientation, events and reorientation sections of recounts. Identify and underline these features in the letter.

- Ask children how this recount differs from the previous two they looked at (e.g. it is written in the first person; it retells events from one viewpoint only; it has a very informal, chatty style; it contains the author's feelings and opinions; it assumes the reader knows the writer). Elicit, if possible, the historical vocabulary in the text. You may need to explain that a **hoplite** was a Greek soldier.

- Ask children who this letter is for (Nicias). Establish that, unlike both other recounts, this one is written for a close friend.

Group follow-up activities

1 red   pupil's book page 24

Children read two extracts and decide which is from a letter and which from a newspaper article. They write down two reasons for each choice.

Guided group support Work with children to focus on clear points of contrast such as layout and opinions/comments.

2 red   pupil's book page 24

Children rewrite a short formal passage as either a letter or as a newspaper article.

3 blue/yellow   pupil's book page 25

Children read extracts from different historical periods. They decide which is from a letter, which from a newspaper and which from a textbook. They give two reasons for each choice.

4 blue/yellow   pupil's book page 26

Children choose one of the extracts and rewrite it in the style of a different recount.

*Guided group support (**blue and yellow**)* Help children to integrate recount and historical fact in an entertaining retelling. If they decide to write a newspaper recount, discuss how the informal elements could be written formally without compromising the journalistic style. If they decide to write a letter, ask children to consider which first person viewpoint they will take.

Plenary   Recap differences between formal, personal and newspaper recounts. Recap similarities (orientation, events and reorientation).

③ Planning a newspaper recount

Objective   To plan a historical event to be written as a newspaper article

Shared session   *You need: OHT/poster 10.*

- Explain to children that they are first going to plan and write about another historical event, as a 'pretend' newspaper recount.

■ Remind children that, as this is a newspaper recount, it is to be written for an unknown audience.

Ensure that the chosen topic offers sufficient scope for two retellings. In subsequent sessions you, and the children, will adapt the recount for a close friend (writing a letter).

■ As a starting point, choose a historical period/episode and ensure children are familiar with the key events. Here are some ideas for writing about the Greeks:
  - famous battles between the Greeks and Persians, such as Marathon (490 BC) or Thermopylai (480 BC);
  - the life of Alexander the Great (356–323 BC);
  - Archimedes's defence of Syracuse against the Romans (215–212 BC).

■ Use OHT/poster 10 to plan your newspaper recount.

■ Plan the orientation section. Recap that it should include a very brief summary of the whole text, as well as brief information about when/who/what/where/why.

■ Plan the main body, or events section. Recap that this will contain key events in chronological order, and will add as many details as possible to hold the reader's interest.

■ Plan the reorientation. Discuss the next major event that happened after your chosen episode, in order to situate the contents even more precisely in time.

■ Now think of a provisional headline to go with your planned newspaper article. Note ideas on the plan.

■ Finally, discuss the type of illustration you will use to accompany the article. Think of a caption to go with it. Make notes on the framework.

Group follow-up activities

1 red   pupil's book page 27   copymaster 9

Children think of a historical event to write about as a newspaper recount. They use the planning framework on copymaster 9.

Guided group support Help children think of an event to write about. Encourage them to talk through their ideas with you and with each other. Remind children to make notes using just a few key words.

2 blue/yellow   pupil's book page 27

Children think of a historical event to write about as a newspaper recount. A list of headings is provided.

Guided group support

Blue Work to ensure that a good level of detail is noted down for the main events section and for the reorientation.

Yellow Discuss different types of journalistic styles – serious, broadsheet-type writing and more chatty and informal tabloid-style writing. Make the point that both styles are for general audiences. Challenge children to choose which style to write their recount in.

Plenary

Collect and display the children's planning frameworks. Discuss the notes they have made and encourage discussion about why. Identify similarities between the work of different groups; isolate any ideas that have occurred only once and explore these further.

Drafting the newspaper recount

Objectives To write about a historical event in the form of a newspaper recount

To write for a general/unknown audience

Shared session *You need: OHT/poster 10 (from Session 3), large sheets of paper.*

*See **Drafting** on page 7 for more detailed guidance on conducting a whole-class drafting session.*

■ Recap the purpose and audience for the newspaper recount you planned in the previous session.

■ Discuss the constraints imposed by writing for an audience we do not know. Explain that, depending on the type of newspaper, journalistic language can be humorous and sensational, or respectable and sensible. Ask children which style they think is more appropriate for an audience they do not know (probably the 'sensible' style).

■ Recap the features of the newspaper recount which you looked at in Session 2 – the use of direct quotes, immediate language and balanced viewpoints.

■ Now draft the newspaper recount, referring constantly to your planning framework.

■ Decide on an attention-grabbing orientation.

■ Move on to the events section. Ask children to think of quotes that relevant people might say about events. Explain that children should try to include a balance of viewpoints.

■ Ask children how you can help the reader understand the sequence of events. Use chronological connectives and, if possible, demonstrate how dates can also be used to show a sequence in historical recount.

■ Ensure the reorientation is both effective and memorable.

■ Discuss what information should go in the headline. Bearing in mind what you have agreed about style, revise the purpose of a headline and elicit some ideas. Can word-play be used to develop and embellish these? Decide on the best suggestion.

Group follow-up activities **red/blue/yellow**

Children draft their own newspaper recounts.

Guided group support

Red Ensure children are working in accordance with their plans. Encourage verbal rehearsals to help establish control of authorial voice. Help children write in paragraphs to show clearly the main sections of the newspaper article.

Blue Ensure paragraphing is used to organise and present events and ideas within the events section.

Yellow Challenge children to use a range of sentence types, switching between complex and simple language for best effect.

Plenary Ask for volunteers to read out any particularly successful sections of text from their drafts. Involve the class in positive and friendly criticism. Encourage children also to read out any parts of their texts they may have been struggling with, so that classmates can give assistance.

(5) Revising and editing the newspaper recount

Objective To improve text according to audience and purpose

Shared session *You need: newspaper article draft (from Session 4), different coloured marker pens.*

*See **Revising and editing** on page 7 for more detailed advice.*

- Display the class draft. Tell children their job is now to read and listen to their draft texts as newspaper readers, and to assess the strengths and weaknesses of their work.

- Make the first revision focus the historical content and vocabulary. Ask children to check the text to ensure that historically accurate words and phrases have been used, where possible. Look for any places that additional historical knowledge could be inserted – perhaps as an aside or in a direct quote.

- Check the structure of the text. Is the headline attention-grabbing and informative? Is the orientation clear and concise? Does it entice the reader to go on? Are the main events related in a logical order?

- Now ask children if they think the language and tone is right for the 'unknown', or general, audience. Remind them that we cannot assume anything about this audience's knowledge of the historical events. Is the text clear and of interest to a general reader? Is there a balance of viewpoints?

Group follow-up activities

Make sure children understand the importance of listening to their partners' texts as general newspaper readers, with no prior knowledge of, or opinions about, the historical event.

red/blue/yellow

Children revise and edit their own texts, working with a partner who can supply the audience response.

Guided group support

Red Help children identify one or two weaknesses in their work.
Blue Take a few sample sentences and rework them for maximum impact.
Yellow Focus on developing control and consistency of style throughout the piece.

Plenary Ask volunteers to read their articles. Enjoy them together. Discuss the 'voice' of each piece and how it was created.

(6) Planning a letter of recount

Objectives To consider the adaptations needed to write about an event for a known audience
To rewrite the newspaper recount as a letter to a friend (a **personal recount**)

Shared session *You need: OHT/poster 11.*

- Tell children they are now going to write a recount of the same historical event as a letter to a close friend.

- Recap the features of this type of recount (written in the first person; retells events from one viewpoint only; informal, chatty style). Refer back to OHT/poster 9, if necessary.

- Discuss ways to write from a single viewpoint. Suggest that children can write about the events as an involved participant or as a casual observer. For example, if the chosen event was the Battle of Marathon, you could write an eyewitness recount as a Persian archer or an Athenian hoplite. Alternatively, you could write as someone living in Athens, worried about the danger facing the city.

- Decide on the viewpoint for the class letter. Now plan it using the framework on OHT/poster 11.

- Plan the orientation. Point out that the aim here is to let the reader know **where** and **when** the events happened, and the writer's relationship to these events.

- Recap the main events recounted in the class newspaper article. Decide on the main events in this letter, from the writer's viewpoint. There may be some big differences! Write a brief note for each event. Check the events are in chronological order.

- Plan the reorientation, possibly referring back to the orientation, or telling the reader what you will do next.

- Decide on an appropriate greeting and closure for the letter.

- Finally, discuss what personal comments and opinions might be included in the letter. Make notes of these on the plan.

Group follow-up activities

1 red   pupil's book page 28   copymaster 10

Children think of a viewpoint for their own recount letter, and plan it using the framework on copymaster 10.

Guided group support Help children to identify a clear point of view for their letters. Ensure planning notes of content and style are sufficiently comprehensive to support future drafting.

2 blue/yellow   pupil's book page 28

Children think of a viewpoint for their own recount letter. They then plan it using headings given in the pupil's book.

Guided group support (***blue and yellow***) As with the red group. Encourage children to include a selection of facts to fit a particular viewpoint.

Plenary

Ask for volunteers from each group to talk about choices they have made, and why. Encourage the class to discuss and comment positively on the thoughts and plans of contributors. Air any lingering doubts or worries about how to approach the task.

 7   Drafting the letter of recount

Objective

To make precise use of language to create an informal, contrasting document

Shared session

You need: OHT/poster 11 (from Session 6), large sheets of paper.

Conduct this session in a similar way to Session 4 (Drafting the newspaper recount), but focusing very explicitly on establishing a contrasting informal, personal tone and incorporating opinion and comment.

- Read through the class letter plan. Recap on the purpose and audience for the letter.

- Now draft the letter together. Expand the orientation. Point out that, as this is a letter to a close friend, it is not so important to write in an attention-grabbing way. It is more important to express personal feelings and opinions.

■ Look at the main events. Ask children to add description and personal detail to each event. Ask them for chronological connectives (and possibly dates) to link the events.

■ Decide whether to add anything to the reorientation.

■ As you draft, encourage children to have fun using informal language, such as slang words and tongue-in-cheek descriptions. Explain that when addressing a familiar audience, their personal voice and style is not only acceptable, but desirable.

■ Incorporate some examples of direct addresses to the intended reader, to achieve the personal tone (e.g. *You should have seen it*; *It was fantastic!*).

■ Keep re-reading the text as it builds to help children hear and maintain control of the first-person, informal voice.

Group follow-up activities   **red/blue/yellow**

Children draft their own recount letters.

Guided group support

Red Ensure that at least some historical vocabulary is used, though not so much as to create too formal a tone. Make sure children remember to include personal details and opinions.

Blue Challenge children to use shorter, less formal sentences to create an authentic personal style. Ensure adequate use of correct historical vocabulary, especially in descriptions.

Yellow Maximise use of historical vocabulary without compromising the informal tone.

Plenary   Share and discuss examples of children's work.

⑧ Revising and editing the letter of recount

Objectives   To check the content and structure of the recount letter

To ensure that the letter is ready for publication

Shared session   *You need: letter draft (from Session 7), different colour marker pens.*

■ Read through the class letter with the children, asking them to listen as if they were the reader, a close friend of the writer. Choose some or all of the following revision focuses to look at together:

    ○ Is the letter written in the first person?

    ○ Does the letter contain opinion and personal comment?

    ○ Is the language appropriate for someone you know well? Can you make it even more personal/conversational?

    ○ Is there accurate historical content and vocabulary?

    ○ Is the sequence of events in a logical order? Is it clear to the reader what has happened?

■ Finish with a check of spelling, grammar and punctuation.

Group follow-up activities   **red/blue/yellow**

Children revise and edit their letters, working with a partner who can supply the audience response.

Guided group support

Red Use textbooks and glossaries to check historical terms are correctly spelled. Ensure all high-frequency words are also correct. Involve children in reading their work aloud to hear whether it makes sense.

Blue Give assistance in the use of commas within sentences to separate ideas. Ensure that all or most sentences are correctly demarcated with capital letters and full stops, even when complex.

Yellow Focus on punctuation as with the blue group. Encourage more able writers to use a widening range of punctuation marks – such as brackets and dashes – especially when inserting personal comments and asides.

Plenary Volunteers discuss the changes they have made to their letters and explain why they have made them. Ask those listening whether they think these amendments have worked.

⑨ Publishing both recounts

Objective To decide how to present the recounts, considering their different layout and different audiences

Shared session *You need: revised newspaper and letter drafts, large sheets of paper, different colour marker pens, ICT facilities (optional), cardboard rolls (optional – see below).*

*1 See **Publishing** on page 8 for more detailed notes on the issues involved in the final presentation of the text.*

2 You may wish to 'publish' this project as a classroom or corridor display. Use contrasting paper colours for the newspaper and letter recounts.

3 This session can be spread over two lessons, one for the newspaper article and one for the letter.

- Involve children in desktop publishing or best handwriting to produce presentation versions of their newspaper articles and letters.

- Discuss how the different audiences for the two recounts might affect presentational choices. As the audience for the newspaper article is unknown, it is best to make the layout as clear and eye-catching as possible, to attract whoever will read it.

- Discuss using a picture to go with the article (this will add interest). What could it show? Where would it go? What sort of caption could go with it?

- For the letter, recap the intended audience and consider the sort of things he/she would like (e.g. use of bright colours and lots of pictures, or a more serious look). Add an address and date to the final letter.

- For the letter, you could use parchment-type paper or involve children in artificially ageing some plain material. Cardboard rolls could be used to make 'scrolls'.

Group follow-up activities   **red/blue/yellow**

Children work on the presentation of their newspaper articles and letters.

Guided group support (all groups) Encourage children to make decisions about the layout of their letters and newspaper articles. Discuss the different presentational devices they can use – ask them why they think these will be effective. Help children to assess their texts from their readers' point of view.

Plenary Display the texts so children can read and comment on each other's work.

ADDITIONAL SESSIONS

Note-making and abbreviations

Objectives

To revise note-making skills

To ensure children are able to make effective notes that are easily read and understood at a later date

To use simple abbreviations in note-making

Shared session   *You need: OHT 12.*

It would be helpful to do this session before the main unit on writing recounts, as children will need to write notes when planning their recounts.

■ Discuss the different purposes for note-making (e.g. making plans for writing; noting key points when researching information, listing cues for a talk).

■ Display OHT 12. Ask children what sort of text this is (a recount) and identify its structure.

■ Tell children they are going to make notes from this text. Ask them to help you cross out unnecessary words until you are left with only key words and important information.

■ Now write notes from this passage.

■ Explain that we can use abbreviations instead of writing out certain words. Ask children if they can spot an abbreviation that is already used in the text (BC = *Before Christ*). Point out that *fourth century* can be written as C4th.

■ Check that these notes contain all the key information in the text.

Group follow-up activities

1 red/blue/yellow   pupil's book page 29

Children match a list of words to standard abbreviations.

2 red   pupil's book page 29

Children write a list of sentences in note form.

Guided group support Help children find and highlight key words in their sentences.

3 blue/yellow   pupil's book page 30

As for activity 2, with a more challenging list of sentences.

Guided group support

Blue Help children reduce their sentences as far as possible without losing meaning. Help them use abbreviations where possible.

Yellow As well as using abbreviations, help children experiment with reducing the longest words to 'word outlines', consisting of the most important consonants and initials. (There is more on this in Term 2, non-fiction focus.)

Plenary

Children swap notes and try to read each other's work. Discuss any problems that have arisen. Ask children what they have learnt about note-making in this session.

Writing and testing instructions

Objectives
To test out and evaluate instructional texts for their effectiveness

To write instructional texts

Shared session
You need: multiple copies of copymaster 11, materials listed on copymaster 11.

Ensure that you have the materials on copymaster 11 in the classroom, but do not assemble them beforehand. This will help revise the importance of providing a 'What you need' section with instructions.

■ Revise what children know about instructional texts (they tell you how to make or do something; they often have two sections, 'What you need' and 'What you have to do'; 'What you have to do' sentences start with a verb and are usually listed one beneath the other).

■ Tell children they are going to test out a set of instructions, to see how easy they are to follow.

■ Divide the class into small groups. Give each group a copy of copymaster 11.

■ Tell children that they are going to make a **pinhole camera**. Explain that this was invented in ancient Greece by Aristotle (around 330 BC), and is the basic idea behind modern television and film.

■ The children work through the instructions in their groups.

■ When they have finished, discuss how the instructions could be improved (e.g. adding a 'What you need' section; explaining that the projected image will be upside down; more diagrams).

■ Explain to children they are going to write and test out some instructions of their own.

Group follow-up activities

Stress that instructions must be followed closely, to evaluate their effectiveness. Children should not be tempted to fill in any 'gaps' in the instructions, but must think how they could be improved.

red/blue/yellow   pupil's book page 31

Working in groups, children either think of their own instructions to write or use the ideas in the pupil's book. They swap their instructions with another group, and evaluate each other's work.

Guided group support

Red Ensure the instructions are in a logical order, and do not miss out any stages.

Blue Encourage children to expand their instructions to make them clearer, adding any extra steps which may help the reader.

Yellow Challenge children to provide clear diagrams to accompany their texts.

Plenary
Discuss how effective each set of instructions is, and how they could be improved. Ask children what they have learnt from this session about writing clear instructions.

Homework suggestions

- Choose a piece of serious historical text from a text-book you have read recently. Rewrite it giving the same facts from a different point of view. Include some comments and opinions. Say which piece you find more interesting. **(After Session 1)**

- Ask two people who were present at the same event to give you separate recounts of this event. Compare their recounts and identify any differences. Can you spot any opinions or comments? **(After Session 2)**

- Rewrite these formal sentences in an informal style. Look at this example to help you:

  Formal: *Children from poor families were often sold as slaves.*

  Informal: *Kids from hard-up families were cashed in as slaves.*

  Greeks believed in many different gods with mighty powers.
  Rich citizens had large homes with many rooms.
  Rich and poor alike spent much of their leisure time watching plays at the amphitheatre.
  The goddess Athena supposedly introduced the olive tree into Greece.
  The flat, round loaves of bread in ancient Greece tended to be coarse and stodgy.
  Usually shown partly naked, Aphrodite was the goddess of love and beauty.
  The hot, dry Greek climate meant that the harvest was often poor and people had little to eat.
  (After Session 3)

- Rewrite these informal sentences in a formal style. Look at this example to help you:

  Informal: *Those boozy Greek guzzlers drank loads of wine.*

  Formal: *Greeks were very fond of wine and drank it in large amounts.*

  The Greeks were really sporty!
  Athletes weren't ashamed of their hunky bodies and took their clothes off for games.
  Clothes were really untrendy! Everyone wore the same boring tunics.
  Greek grub was great! They noshed fruit, yoghurt, meat and cheese all the time!
  For storing oil and stuff they used a fancy vase sort of thing called an amphora.
  A girl's dad would pick out a hubby for her when she was about twelve.
  When he got to twelve a boy was all grown up and couldn't keep his toys any more. He had to promise them to the god Apollo.
  (After Session 4)

- In past times, slaves often looked after their owners' children. If the children were naughty they often blamed the slaves, who were punished instead of them. The slaves were not allowed to speak up in their own defence. Think of an incident – like an ornament being broken – that a Greek master might have blamed a slave for. Write a letter recounting this incident from the slave's point of view and from the master's. **(After Session 6)**

- Ask a friend to record on tape a short recount of something he or she has done recently. Play the tape back and try to write down exactly what you hear. Don't leave anything out. Now look at what you have written. Is it anything like the informal texts you have been reading with your teacher? What are the differences?

  Get two friends to ask you simple questions about your history topic. Give one friend factual answers. Give the other friend facts too, but try to entertain him or her by giving your answers in a funny way. Write a brief report about the facts you gave and the reactions of your two audiences.

  Ask a friend or relative to identify one adult and one child you both know well. Choose a simple topic. Write two short recounts of this topic, a formal one for the adult and an informal one for the child. Record these on a tape and play them back to yourself. If the two recounts do not sound different enough, try again. When you're happy with the results, play the tape to your intended audience.
  (After Session 7)

UNIT 2 How to write a recount for two different audiences

Colour the right number of stars to show how well you did the following things:

0 stars = I didn't do it.
1 star = I gave it a try.
2 stars = I did it quite well.

3 stars = I did it well.
4 stars = I did an excellent job!

I made a clear difference between formal and informal language.	☆	☆	☆	☆
I wrote and punctuated some complex sentences.	☆	☆	☆	☆
I used appropriate historical vocabulary.	☆	☆	☆	☆
I had fun with the informal style!	☆	☆	☆	☆
I learnt how to use literacy skills to show my historical knowledge.	☆	☆	☆	☆
I know how to use recounts for a range of purposes and audiences.	☆	☆	☆	☆
I created two different 'voices' in my writing.	☆	☆	☆	☆

Something I am especially pleased with

Something my audience liked in my writing

Something I'd like to do better next time

Term two fiction focus:
3 How to write a legend

What most children will already know:

The purpose of beginnings in fiction
How to describe settings
How to describe characters
The role of problems and resolutions in driving plot
How to use key words in note-making and planning

What children will learn in this unit:

The style and structure of legends
Themes that legends often contain
How to think creatively about resolutions to problems
How to match settings to the characters that live there
How to consider the needs of the reader in their writing

 Beginnings and settings in legends

Objectives
To understand what information goes at the beginning of legends

To think about setting, and words and phrases to describe it

Shared session
You need: OHT/poster 13 (see below for where to mask the text), a large sheet of paper.

■ Tell children you are going to read three words from a story. Can they tell if these words come from the beginning, middle or end of the story? Do they know what kind of story this might be? Read the first three words on OHT/poster 13 (*Long, long ago*).

■ Write up the name *Odysseus*. What do children know about him? Explain that he is the hero of a Greek legend. Revise children's knowledge of legends (they are traditional tales, usually about heroes or heroines, that come from all over the world).

■ Revise story beginnings, eliciting the information these usually contain (characters, setting, problem). Explain that story beginnings can also tell us both <u>when</u> and <u>why</u> things happened.

■ Tell children you are going to read the beginning of one of Odysseus's adventures. As you read, ask them to think about four things:

  ○ **when** this story takes place;
  ○ **where** it happens;
  ○ **who** the characters are;
  ○ **why** they are there.

■ Read OHT/poster 13, up to *...the ground began to shake*. Mask the rest of the text.

■ Ask children about the four things they listened out for.

> **When:** a long time ago. This setting is in the non-specific distant past, in common with most legends.
> **Where:** an island
> **Who:** Odysseus and his men
> **Why:** Odysseus and his men are trying to find their way home after fighting in a long war.

■ Ask children how the setting makes them feel. Ask them to identify words or phrases that evoke these feelings (e.g. *lonely seas, towering cliffs*).

■ Explain that legends usually have strong ideas, or **themes**, running through the story, such as cunning versus stupidity, or perseverance through danger. Discuss themes in other legends children have read. Discuss what might be the theme of this legend.

Group follow-up activities

1 red   pupil's book page 32

Children read the beginning of a Siberian legend (retold in *The Weather Drum* by Rosalind Kerven). They answer 'when, where, who and why' questions.

Guided group support Reinforce the structure of beginnings by identifying each aspect in the text provided. Children could then discuss alternatives to any one of these features (e.g. change <u>where</u> it happened).

2 red   pupil's book page 32

Children write about how the setting makes them feel. They write down words or phrases which they consider powerful.

3 blue/yellow   pupil's book page 33

Children read passages from versions of *Theseus and the Minotaur* and *Beowulf*. They write how the settings make them feel, identifying words or phrases which they consider powerful.

*Guided group support (**blue**)* Help children examine the effect on the reader of the descriptive language used to describe settings in other legends. Discuss alternative words and the effect these would create.

4 blue/yellow   pupil's book page 33

Children use other sources of information (books of the legends, websites, encyclopaedia) to answer 'when, where, who and why' questions about the legends.

*Guided group support (**yellow**)* Help children identify main and subsidiary themes in short legends. Begin a chart of themes in legends (for use in later sessions).

Plenary

Make a poster, entitled 'How to write a legend'. Ask children for 'when, where, who and why' information from the legends in their activities. Write this on the poster under a 'Beginnings' sub-heading. Discuss with children any powerful words they identified in their extracts. Write these on the poster under the sub-heading 'Settings'.

If time, return to the last line you read on OHT/poster 13, *Suddenly the ground began to shake*. Ask children to think about what is causing this, and to be prepared to discuss their ideas at the beginning of the next session.

② Describing characters

Objectives

To look at words and phrases that describe an extraordinary character

To look at features of an extraordinary character that children can reproduce in their own writing

Shared session *You need: OHT/poster 13, class poster (from Session 1).*

■ Re-read briefly the section of OHT/poster 13 which you looked at in Session 1. Ask children what they think causes the ground to shake.

- Read the next line only: *Something big was approaching*. Explain that in this legend, Odysseus meets a huge creature called the Cyclops.

- Recap your discussion of themes in Session 1. Now that children have more information about the legend, ask what they think the theme might be (e.g. good versus evil).

- Divide the class into two groups. Tell children that you are going to read the next part of the story. As you read, they should look for words and phrases that tell them:
  - what the Cyclops looked like (*first group*);
  - how the Cyclops behaved (*second group*).

- Read the rest of OHT/poster 13. Then ask children to discuss the words they noticed with a partner. Collect suggestions and underline them on the OHT/poster.

- Ask what each word or phrase tells us about the Cyclops, in terms of its size, strange features, sounds, actions or powers. Copy the table below and fill in the 'Size' column as an example, writing key words only and reminding children about note-making. Elicit words and phrases for the other columns. Ask which words we can leave out when we are making notes.

Size	Strange features	Sounds	Actions	Powers
as big as mountain	single massive eye	laugh like great crack of thunder	stomped	strength (rolled massive boulder)
enormous mouth			rolled massive boulder	size (grabbed two men)
			grabbed two men	
			tossed them into mouth	

Group follow-up activities

1 red   pupil's book page 34

Children draw a character chart as modelled in the shared session. They fill it in using a description of character from *The Weather Drum*. (N.B. Children will not be able to complete the sounds column from the text, but can use their imagination to do so.)

Guided group support Help children identify how <u>each</u> extraordinary feature of a character plays an important part in the story (e.g. the Cyclops's size meant that he could easily grab the men and toss them into his cavernous mouth).

2 red   pupil's book page 34

Children use their table to draw and label a picture of the character.

3 blue   pupil's book page 34

As for activity 1, but noting down features of two characters described on page 35.

Guided group support Help children identify how **challenges** are created in legends (e.g. by making links between a character's extraordinary features and the problems each of these causes).

4 yellow   pupil's book page 34

As for activity 1, but noting down features of all three characters described on page 35.

Guided group support Reinforce understanding of the **purpose** of a character's extraordinary features in a legend (i.e. as the main factor in causing a sequence of events).

5 blue/yellow   pupil's book page 35

Children choose one of the characters in their table, and draw and label a picture of it.

Plenary   Ask children for the words and phrases they have found. Return to your 'Legends' poster. Write the best suggestions under the heading 'Character', retaining the categories of size, strange features, sounds, actions and powers.

③ Problems and resolutions in legends

Objective   To think creatively about ways to solve problems

Shared session   *You need: OHTs/posters 13 and 14.*

■ Ask children what problem the Cyclops was causing Odysseus and his men – return to OHT/poster 13 if necessary. (The Cyclops has trapped the Greeks in his cave.)

■ Explain that Odysseus came up with a clever plan to solve this problem. He waited until the Cyclops had drunk so much wine he fell asleep.

■ Now read OHT/poster 14, up to ...*the Greeks couldn't escape*. Mask the rest of the text.

■ Establish what Odysseus has done to the Cyclops (blinded him). Elicit the problem that still faces Odysseus and his men (still trapped in the cave).

■ Discuss what Odysseus could do to solve this problem. In response to ideas, point out further problems, starting with the phrase *But what if...?* Develop a refrain, going around the class – for example:

  – *They could sneak past the Cyclops.*

  – *But what if he saw them?*

  – *They could dig a tunnel out of the cave.*

  – *But what if they didn't have any spades?*

■ Tell children to look out for Odysseus's solution as you read the rest of OHT/poster 14. When you have finished, ask children to identify where the solution is mentioned in the text, and underline this.

■ Finally, return to the theme of the legend. Have the children changed their opinion about the theme? What do they think it is now?

Group follow-up activities   **1 red   pupil's book page 36**

Children copy out a simple problem/resolution table in their book. They write down the problem in the Big Raven legend and what they think is the resolution – it involves one of the objects pictured in the pupil's book.

Guided group support   Identify how problems can have a range of different resolutions by discussing alternative resolutions to the main problem in a simple legend.

2 blue   pupil's book page 36

As for activity 1, with the Theseus legend – the resolution involves two of the objects pictured.

Guided group support Reinforce understanding of themes in legends by recapping the main theme of the Odysseus legend. Help children identify the main themes in other short legends. Discuss common themes. Add these to class chart started with the yellow group in Session 1.

3 yellow   pupil's book page 36

As for activity 1, with the Perseus legend – the resolution involves three of the objects pictured.

Guided group support Identify the use of problems and resolutions as events unfold in legends. Discuss the purpose of these (e.g. to show how the hero or heroine perseveres beyond the first setback).

4 red   pupil's book page 37   copymaster 12

Children use a storyboard illustrating problem and resolution in the Cyclops legend. They cut up copymaster 12 and rearrange the captions beneath the pictures.

5 blue/yellow   pupil's book page 37

As activity 4, but children write captions for each picture in the pupil's book.

Plenary   Discuss how the problems in the three legends are resolved. First of all, find out if any children have read any of the legends and therefore know the correct answer. Ask for resolutions from children who have <u>not</u> read the full version of their legend, followed by those who have.

 Planning characters and setting

Objectives   To invent further extraordinary characters and their features

To see how words are added to make descriptions more exciting

To think of appropriate settings for these extraordinary characters

Shared session   *You need: class poster (from Session 2).*

- Tell children they are going to write a new legend for Odysseus. Establish an audience for this story.

- Explain that you are going to invent another extraordinary character Odysseus met on his journey home. Recap the main features of the Cyclops – his size, strange features, sounds, actions and powers.

- Ask children to think about these five things for the new character. Give them time to discuss ideas with a partner. They can use the 'Character' section of your 'Legends' poster to help them.

- Collect ideas for each category and decide on the best ones. Discuss how words can be added to make descriptions more exciting. Use an example and show children how to extend it. For example, *three long tongues* could become *three long black tongues, like thrashing whips*. Add descriptions to the class poster.

- Now recap the place where the Cyclops lived. Ask why this is a good place for the Cyclops to live (e.g. the massive rocks, cliffs and caves match his size). Explain that settings in legends are often suited to the characters that live there (e.g. Medusa's island; Mount Olympus). Ask children to think of other examples from their reading.

■ Discuss the place where your new character might live. Refer to the 'Settings' section of the class poster for ideas. Ask children for exciting or interesting adjectives to describe this place. Again, add these to the class poster.

Group follow-up activities

1 red/blue/yellow   pupil's book page 38   copymaster 13

Children think of their own extraordinary characters and settings to match. They use the copymaster to plan the features of their characters, and to write about what they can see, hear, smell, etc. in their settings.

Guided group support

Red Help children develop appropriate settings for their extraordinary characters. Help them to explore ideas about setting by pretending to be their characters and boast about their homes to a partner (e.g. *the nastiest thing is...; the most dangerous thing is...; the most frightening thing is...; the best thing is...*).

Blue Help children invent a character with extraordinary features and identify what events these features cause. Help them identify why their settings are appropriate for their characters by looking at each feature and explaining how this suits the character.

Yellow Help children decide, as their extraordinary characters, what they want to be able to do and how they want their visitors to feel. Help children choose appropriate features to be able to do this. Discuss how choice of vocabulary can help the reader to experience similar feelings to those of the visitors.

2 red/blue/yellow   pupil's book page 38   copymaster 13 (completed)

Children use their plan (on copymaster 13) to draw and label a picture of their character in his or her setting.

Plenary Ask children to describe their settings to the rest of the class. Ask those listening to close their eyes during these descriptions and think about how the characters and places make them feel.

5 Planning the legend

Objectives To plan the story development of a new legend

To consider how a conclusion to a story can be added after the resolution

Shared session *You need: OHT/poster 15, class poster (from Session 4).*

The plan is designed to let you substitute an alternative hero/heroine for Odysseus, if you wish.

■ Tell children you are now going to plan the new legend for Odysseus.

■ Use OHT/poster 15. With children's help, fill in the first three parts of the beginning section ('Hero/heroine', 'Extraordinary character' and 'Setting'). Revise note-making as you write – use key words only.

■ Recap the problem that faced Odysseus in the Cyclops legend, the events in that story and the resolution.

■ Discuss the extraordinary character you created in Session 4. What problems might it cause Odysseus? Consider how its special features could cause particular problems. Use the class poster to help you.

■ List suggestions and decide on the best one. Add this to the beginning section of OHT/poster 15, under 'Problem'.

■ Now ask children how Odysseus could trick your extraordinary character. Follow the same procedure as before, writing the key words in the ending section of the plan, under 'Resolution'.

■ Now work backwards and plan the events in the story, before the problem is resolved. Encourage children to build these events up to a climax, before the resolution.

■ Finally, ask children what happens at the end of the Cyclops legend (the Cyclops calls on his father, the sea god Poseidon, to attack Odysseus's ship with a storm). Explain that this is the **conclusion** to the legend – the result is that Odysseus's ship is driven further off course. Plan a conclusion to your legend and add it to the ending section of the plan.

Group follow-up activities

Reduce the number of events given on copymaster 14 according to the needs of this group.

1 red   pupil's book page 39   copymaster 14

Children use a supportive framework to plan their legends.

Guided group support Help children identify the problem for the hero or heroine and ask how they would solve it.

2 blue/yellow   pupil's book page 39

Children copy out the framework in the pupil's book and use it to plan their legends.

Guided group support

Blue Focus on what happens after the resolution of the problem (i.e. the conclusion). Ask children why this is important.

Yellow Help children identify the most exciting part of their legends. Discuss the purpose of this climax for the characters involved (their most testing challenge), and the purpose for the readers (it keeps them intrigued as to how the characters will overcome a seemingly impossible situation).

Plenary

Ask for volunteers to read out their plans. Ask those listening to refer to the class plan to make sure all the elements have been included.

6 Drafting the legend

Objective

To turn plans into draft legends

Shared session

You need: OHT/poster 15, large sheets of paper, OHTs/posters 13 and 14 (optional).

*See **Drafting** on page 7 for more detailed advice on conducting a whole-class drafting session.*

■ Read through your legend plan with the class.

■ Ask children what they think are the themes of this new legend. Make some decisions about how to show these themes in the shared writing. If necessary, return to OHTs/posters 13 and 14 to see how Odysseus's cunning and perseverance, as well as the Cyclops' evil, are portrayed.

■ Before drafting the beginning, recap the 'when, where, who, why' information contained at the start of the Cyclops legend. Include all this information in your draft.

■ As you draft the legend, refer back to the plan to ensure that all the information has been included.

■ Remind children that plans contain only the key words. Ask them to help you turn notes into full sentences.

Group follow-up activities　**red/blue/yellow**

Children use their plans to draft their own legends.

Guided group support

Red Reinforce children's understanding of themes in legends by discussing opposites in relation to their extraordinary characters and the heroes or heroines (e.g. opposites in behaviour, abilities, nature, appearance).

Blue Focus on the choice of descriptive words or phrases to help stir strong feelings and create vivid pictures for readers. Discuss the possible effect of choices on readers.

Yellow Focus on the use of cliff-hangers to help build tension in a story.

Plenary　Ask for volunteers to read out their draft legends. Set the class different listening targets:

Red: think about the characters and setting.
Blue: think about the themes in the legend.
Yellow: think about the conclusion. Does it reflect the theme of the legend? Can you think of a way to improve it?

7　Revising and editing the legend

Objectives　To improve writing by returning to it and doing further work

To consider the main points about legends and ensure these are included in children's own work

Shared session　*You need: legend draft, large sheets of paper.*

See **Revising and editing** on page 7 for more detailed advice.

■ Display the draft of the class legend. Recap on the intended audience. Choose some or all of the following revision focuses, and decide how to meet the needs of the audience for each one.

　　◉　How well has the theme(s) of this legend been brought out? How could it be made clearer?

　　◉　Remind the class of the descriptive language of legends and, where needed, ask them to help you extend descriptions of place and character.

　　◉　Use a thesaurus to find synonyms which make descriptions more interesting.

　　◉　Look at the problem and resolution. Does the resolution overcome <u>all</u> the problems? If necessary, repeat the *But what if...?* refrain from Session 3.

■ Finish with a check of spelling, grammar and punctuation.

Group follow-up activities　**red/blue/yellow**

Children revise and edit their legends.

Guided group support

Red Focus on adding words or phrases to their legends to emphasise the extraordinary character's features and to make the setting match the character.

Blue Focus on the use of a variety of connectives at the beginnings of paragraphs.

Yellow Focus on the use of punctuation to emphasise important points or to create desired effects (e.g. ellipses, dashes, exclamation marks).

Plenary Children read their completed legends to a partner, and receive feedback on:

- how easy it is to follow the plot (the problem, events and climax, and resolution);
- how well the text flows;
- the features of legends contained in each text.

If time, pairs feed back to the whole class.

8 Publishing the legend

Objectives To consider the variety of ways a text can be improved before publication

To appreciate the completion of a project, from planning to publication

Shared session *You need: child's legend draft, sheets of A4 or A5 paper, different coloured marker pens, ICT facilities (optional).*

*See **Publishing** on page 8 for more detailed notes on the issues involved in the final presentation of the text.*

- Use one of the children's legend drafts. Explain that you are going to see how to present a finished version of this story.

- Decide how many pages you will need for the legend. Mark which sections should start on each page. Use new sheets of paper, and add page numbers accordingly. Tell children they will need to copy out neatly, or word-process their legends.

- Make notes about illustrations on the new sheets of paper. Discuss where the illustration of the character and setting (from Session 4) could go. Are further illustrations needed?

- Discuss the cover for the book. Decide on a title, and an appropriate illustration.

- Think of a blurb for the back cover. Discuss what information this should include (e.g. story synopsis; description of the type of reader who will enjoy the story).

Group follow-up activities **red/blue/yellow**

The children work on the final presentation of their legends.

Guided group support

Red Help children plan the layout of their legends bearing in mind the effects on the reader – for example, which parts of the legend lend themselves to being on a new page in order to act as a cliff-hanger.

Blue Focus on the style and purpose of the blurb. Help children choose some exciting sentences, followed by an enticing question to the reader.

Yellow Identify how different textual features can be used to add emphasis at key points in the story (e.g. italics, bold, capital letters, different fonts, different size print).

Plenary Ask children to identify any difficulties they had in publishing their legends. Discuss how these could be resolved. Ask children to show/read their legend to a partner, who provides feedback on the overall presentation.

ADDITIONAL SESSIONS

Writing a poem to accompany the legend

Objective   To write new poems based on a model

Shared session   *You need: OHT/poster 16, OHT/poster 17 (optional).*

- Recap the conclusion of Odysseus and the Cyclops. Ask children how they think the Cyclops felt at the end of the story.

- Tell children you are going to read a poem in which the Cyclops asks Poseidon to help him get revenge on Odysseus.

- Read OHT/poster 16 to the class. Explain, if necessary, that in Greek legend, *Charybdis* was a terrible whirlpool that sucked in ships which came too near.

- Read lines 5–8 again, stressing the repeated words. Ask children how the repetition adds to the effect (e.g. it emphasises the Cyclops's rage). Ask for other examples of repetition in the poem.

- Now tell children they are going to write a new revenge poem for the class extraordinary character to use against Odysseus. If you wish, you can use OHT/poster 17 as a framework, brainstorming words to go in the blank spaces.

- When you have finished, read through the new version of the poem with children. Ask them to imagine how the extraordinary character is feeling as it says this poem. Ask children to express this in their reading – without causing chaos!

Group follow-up activities   **1 red/blue   pupil's book page 40**

Children copy out the framework, and complete a revenge poem for their own extraordinary characters to say.

Guided group support

Red Help children think about the feelings of the Cyclops towards Odysseus. Discuss how their extraordinary characters might feel about Odysseus at the end of their legends. Identify the thoughts that would be in the character's mind (e.g. revenge).

Blue Help children consider the audience and purpose of the words. Discuss how their character might speak to a power from whom they are seeking help. Discuss words that would best elicit this help.

2 yellow   pupil's book page 40

Children make up a new revenge poem for their extraordinary character to say.

Guided group support Focus on the use of repetition to emphasise two important aspects of the extraordinary character's responses (e.g. praising the power from whom help is sought and seeking a particular form of revenge).

Plenary   Volunteers read out their new poems. Ask those listening if they can identify any repetition in these poems.

Matching writing to the needs of the reader

Objectives

To match writing to the needs of an identified reader

To familiarise children with the layout and style of postcards

Shared session *You need: assortment of postcards (see below), copymaster 15 (enlarged), marker pens.*

For homework before this session, ask children to bring postcards into school.

- Look at any postcards you and/or children have brought into school. Discuss favourite ones, and establish that we often send postcards when we are on holiday, showing the places we have visited.

- Explain that Odysseus had a wife called Penelope, back home in Greece. You are going to write a postcard to Penelope, describing the place you, as Odysseus, have just arrived at.

- Using the enlarged version of copymaster 15, demonstrate the features of a postcard, with the address on the right-hand side, the greeting and closure. Discuss suitable greetings and signings-off. Establish whether a formal or informal tone is appropriate.

- Write the postcard with the children. The class legend plan may or may not be used, as appropriate. Remind the children that Odysseus is writing this, so use *I* not *he*, and change the verb endings.

- Discuss the needs of the reader. What information would Penelope want to hear about this place? Would she want to know that Odysseus was in danger? Remember to include personal details, as the reader is someone very close to the writer!

- Finally, fill in the address. Revise the order in which an address is written (receiver's name, house name/number, street, town, country, postcode).

Group follow-up activities

1 red/blue/yellow pupil's book page 41 copymaster 15

Children use a framework to write a postcard to an identified reader (Penelope is suggested in the pupil's book). Children can draw the setting on the other side of their copy of the copymaster (as the picture on the postcard).

Guided group support

Red Focus on the type of personal details that could be included on a postcard. Help children think of one or two parts of the Odysseus legend where personal details could be written (e.g. an incident that happened to Odysseus as he climbed the rocky path to the cave).

Blue Help children consider the decisions a character may make about what to include or exclude by considering the effects of details on the receiver.

Yellow Help children to consider the possible effects on the receiver where key points have <u>not</u> been mentioned in the message (e.g. what might Penelope think if Odysseus said nothing about the inhabitants of the island?). Discuss how Odysseus could overcome this problem (e.g. by underplaying the facts rather than lying).

Plenary

Ask for volunteers to read out their postcards. Ask children how they think Penelope/the intended reader would feel on reading them!

Homework suggestions

- Find out more about Odysseus. Find answers to these questions:
  - Who was Odysseus?
  - How long ago did he live?
  - When were the legends written?
  - Where are they set?
- Use as many sources of information as you can (e.g. books about Odysseus, a version of Homer's *The Odyssey*, encyclopaedias and websites). **(After Session 1)**
- Write the Cyclops's diary for the day Odysseus landed. Describe how he first became aware of the visitors, what he thought and felt when he first saw them, and what he planned to do. **(After Session 2)**
- Choose a story (preferably a legend) that you know well. Draw a chart to show the main problem and resolution. Next, think of an alternative resolution to the story. Try to think of a resolution that fits with all that has happened in the story **(After Session 3)**

- Write some sentences describing the weather at different points in the story, to match these different situations: when Odysseus first landed; when the Cyclops first appeared; when Odysseus's boat sailed away from the island. **(After Session 4)**
- Write a poem in similar style to 'The Cyclops' Revenge', to be said by Odysseus's men, thanking him for saving them. This poem should include:
  - words of address;
  - praise for Odysseus's qualities;
  - good wishes for his future.

  (After 'Writing a poem to accompany the legend')
- Find some used postcards and bring them into school. Try to find ones that show different settings. Think about the writer and reader of each postcard. How well do they know each other? Can you tell this from the postcard? **(Before 'Matching writing to the needs of the reader')**

UNIT 3 How to write a legend

Colour the right number of stars to show how well you did the following things:

0 stars = I didn't do it.   3 stars = I did it well.
1 star   = I gave it a try.   4 stars = I did an excellent job!
2 stars = I did it quite well.

I thought of a main theme for a legend.	☆	☆	☆	☆
I planned an extraordinary creature for a legend.	☆	☆	☆	☆
I planned a setting that matched the extraordinary character of a legend.	☆	☆	☆	☆
I used descriptive language to help the reader to picture the setting and character.	☆	☆	☆	☆
I planned a legend that contained problems and resolutions.	☆	☆	☆	☆
I wrote a conclusion to a legend.	☆	☆	☆	☆
I improved my writing by revising it.	☆	☆	☆	☆
I presented my legend in an interesting way.	☆	☆	☆	☆

Something I am especially pleased with

Something my audience liked in my writing

Something I'd like to do better next time

Term two non-fiction focus:
4 How to write a non-chronological report with explanation

What most children will already know:

Non-chronological reports provide information about a specific subject

They present information in logically organised sections

They often use present tense verbs and plural nouns

They feature 'technical' or subject specific vocabulary

They sometimes incorporate an annotated diagram

What children will learn in this unit:

How to write clearly and concisely

More about writing in an impersonal style

How to incorporate features of explanatory text within a non-chronological report

How to record and acknowledge sources

More about organising information into logical sections with headings and bullet points

More about incorporating technical vocabulary and writing a glossary

 Analysing key features

Objectives
To consolidate understanding and application of the three-part framework

To give practice in presenting, sequencing and categorising information

Shared session
You need: OHTs/posters 18 and 19, copymasters 16, 17 and 18, six large cards (see below), a large sheet of paper for class poster.

- Before the lesson starts, you may wish to write these six extra facts on large cards.
  1 The planets have no light of their own, but shine by reflected sunlight.
  2 The Sun's diameter is 864,000 miles.
  3 Our solar system may have come from condensation from a cloud of gas and dust in space.
  4 The planets are tiny compared with the Sun.
  5 The hottest planet in the solar system is Venus.
  6 The Sun is so bright that it is not safe to look directly at it.

- Tell children that they are going to write a non-chronological report. First, they will read a text to help them remember the main features. Display and read 'The Solar System' on OHTs/posters 18 and 19.

- Give children two minutes, in pairs, to answer the following questions:

  – What tells you that this is a non-chronological report text?

  – What is the purpose of the text?

  – How is it organised?

- Take feedback. As each feature is identified, annotate OHTs/posters 18 and 19. Make sure the following points are covered (but note that you will go into the language features in more detail in Session 2):

Purpose: to provide information; to describe and classify things.

Structure: recap on the three-part framework: opening section, main section and closing section. (Box these in different colours.)

Opening section: defines and introduces the subject. (Compare its length with that of the main section.)

Main section: presents facts. (Ask children how a main section is organised and why – headings and sub-headings are used to separate different parts and make the text clearer.) Point out that a piece of explanatory text may be included within a non-chronological report – for example, paragraph 3, which explains how the Sun produces light and heat. (Ask children why explanation is sometimes included within a report – it helps the reader to understand why or how something happens.)

Closing section: includes a fascinating fact or a brief summary.

Other features of non-chronological reports:
– annotated diagram (supports the written information in a visual format, which readers may find more accessible);
– list of sources (ask where the writer found the information in the report and look at how source material is acknowledged);
– use of bullet points;
– language features such as use of present tense and subject-specific vocabulary.

■   Explain that you have found six extra facts on the solar system. Display or read out one of the cards, asking where this information would fit best into the report. Encourage class discussion and continue until all six facts are incorporated into the text. Here is a possible solution:

1   *The planets have no light...* under 'The planets' perhaps after line 4 (after *...in orbit around some of the planets.*).
2   *The Sun's diameter...* under 'The Sun' perhaps after line 1 (after *... medium brightness and average size.*).
3   *Our solar system...* under 'The solar system' perhaps after line 7 (after *... about 4.6 billion years ago*).
4   *The planets are tiny...* under 'The planets' perhaps after line 2 (after *... in elliptical orbits.*).
5   *The hottest planet...* under the bullet point for Venus (perhaps reword *as the brightest and hottest planet...*).
6   *The Sun is so bright...* under 'The Sun', perhaps after line 1 (after *... medium brightness and average size.*).

Group follow-up activities

1 red   pupil's book page 42   copymaster 16

Children copy the headings used in 'The Solar System' text on to the framework on copymaster 16. They then look at the six extra facts in the pupil's book and write each under the appropriate heading.

Guided group support Work with children to consolidate understanding of the three-part framework. Help them understand that report writers have to organise information logically. Focus on the fact that a paragraph contains related ideas and information, and is labelled appropriately.

2 blue   pupil's book page 43   copymaster 17

Children cut up the copymaster and group the statements according to the three-part framework. Once children are happy they have arranged them appropriately, they paste them on a blank sheet of paper, correctly ordered, and write in the headings they have decided on. (You may wish to return to this in the next session, for further work on using pronouns and linking sentences.)

Guided group support Consolidate understanding of paragraphs as with the red group. Establish the link between effective paragraphing and clarity. Help children appreciate the benefits of clear organisation.

3 yellow   pupil's book page 43   copymasters 17 and 18

Children cut up both copymasters and group the statements according to the three-part framework. They then identify the key words in each section and use these to create clear headings.

Guided group support As with the blue group. Make sure children understand the importance of identifying key words in choosing appropriate headings.

Plenary Begin a class poster summarising the key features of reports with explanation. Recap on key features, including:

- three-part structure;
- headings;
- bullet points/numbered points with logically arranged information;
- annotated diagrams;
- acknowledgement of sources.

Keep the poster for use in future sessions.

2 How to make text clear and concise

Objectives To identify language features that aid clarity and conciseness

To recognise how subject-specific key words are used in non-chronological reports

Shared session *You need: OHTs/posters 18 and 19, class poster (from Session 1).*

- Tell children that they are going to learn how to write reports in clear, concise language.

- Display and re-read OHTs/posters 18 and 19.

- Ask children to identify and underline examples of key language features, asking how each is used to help the reader. Focus on the following points:

- **Headings, sub-headings and bullet points** are usually brief and often use key words from the text. (Help the reader to see how the text is organised and to identify most important information.)

- **Sentences** are direct, and often short and to the point. (To give information as clearly and simply as possible.)

- Use of **pronouns** (e.g. *it, its, they*) and **connectives** (e.g. *and, as a result*). (To link ideas and help make the text more concise.) Ask children to recap on other linking words and phrases they know that are used in explanatory text to show cause and effect (e.g. *so, therefore, consequently*).

- Use of **subject-specific vocabulary** (e.g. *photosphere, X-rays*). (The author needs to use scientific terms that are not usual in everyday conversation in order to be clear and accurate about the subject matter.)

■ Use of a **glossary** (helps the reader to understand subject-specific vocabulary. Without it, authors could not write concisely because they would have to use lengthy explanations.) Can children find any other words that could usefully have been included in the glossary?

■ Use of **present tense** (most of the text is in the present tense because it describes facts that are generally true *now* – at the time of writing).

Group follow-up activities

1 red/blue   pupil's book page 44

Children match words with glossary definitions then write some definitions of their own.

2 red   pupil's book page 45

Children rewrite a text using pronouns and connectives to make it more readable.

Guided group support Remind children that the use of pronouns (*it, they*, etc.) avoids repetition and makes writing more concise. Point out that pronouns must be used with care so that the main subject of each sentence remains clear.

3 blue   pupil's book page 45   copymaster 16

Children return to the text that they sequenced in the previous session (from copymaster 17) and fill in the information on copymaster 16. They then try to link the sentences, where appropriate, using pronouns and connectives.

Guided group support Encourage children to combine sentences <u>where appropriate</u>. Encourage them to use pronouns to avoid repeating the key words (e.g. *it, they, its*).

4 yellow   pupil's book page 46

Ask children to re-order the jumbled sentences correctly. They then add headings for each section and a title for the whole passage.

Guided group support Challenge children to identify the points at which the focus changes. Help them to make informed decisions about how text should be divided and labelled for clarity and to meet readers' needs.

*Guided group support (**all groups**)* Make sure children appreciate the advantages of using correct technical terms. Help them to feel confident rather than self-conscious about this. Discuss the challenges to the reader in coping with subject-specific vocabulary, and the support offered by a glossary.

Plenary

Ask children to contribute ideas on how to make a report clearer and more concise. Add this information to the class poster. Recap on key features, including: technical vocabulary, glossary, pronouns and connectives, simple and direct language, use of the present tense.

③ Writing in an impersonal, formal style

Objective

To reinforce earlier sessions on writing in an impersonal, formal style and to provide further practice

Shared session   *You need: OHT/poster 20.*

■ Remind children of the convention that report texts are **formal** and **impersonal**.

- Display and read OHT/poster 20, asking children to look out for examples of appropriate/inappropriate words and sentences. Underline these, using one colour for <u>appropriate</u> and another for <u>inappropriate</u> elements. Challenge children to explain <u>why</u> these examples of language are appropriate or inappropriate.

- Help children by reading parts of the text aloud and asking how it sounds – like a formal lecture or a chat with a friend?

- Ask children to suggest rewording for parts of the text that they consider inappropriate.

Group follow-up activities

1 red   pupil's book page 47

Children read sentences and decide which are appropriate for a report. They then rewrite the inappropiate sentences (2, 3, 5 and 7) in a more formal style.

Guided group support Encourage children to focus on the 'voice' of each sentence and imagine it belonging to a person. Stress that the authorial voice of a report is formal and impersonal.

2 blue   pupil's book page 48

Children work in pairs to edit a paragraph of text about Jupiter, eliminating inappropriate language elements

Guided group support Recap the ideas covered in the shared session and challenge children to apply what they have learnt.

3 yellow   pupil's book page 49

Children are given some key facts and vocabulary from which they construct a section from a formal report.

Guided group support Focus on the language that must be added around the facts in order to present them in a coherent and appropriate style.

Plenary

Ask children to talk about what and how they have learnt about report writing. Help them to summarise what they consider to be the most important points.

4 Planning the non-chronological report

Objectives

To plan a text with a particular audience in mind

To adapt and refine a basic structure for a particular purpose

To make a detailed plan for a longer text

Shared session   *You need: OHT/poster 21, copymaster 16.*

- Explain that you are going to demonstrate how to plan a non-chronological report and that the children will then plan reports of their own.

- Decide on a topic for your report, possibly something related to another subject the children are studying. Identify the intended audience and means of publication.

- Using the framework on OHT/poster 21, ask children to suggest basic content for each of the three main sections.

- Write their suggestions for the opening section without modification if possible. Decide how best to state what the report is about. Decide whether any additional information is needed to make this clear to the audience.

While planning the main section, put to one side any material that might be used in the closing section. Encourage children to help you identify such material.

- Next, discuss how you might best organise the main section. What do children know about the topic? How should this information be presented? Remind children that the report must be interesting for the audience.

- Ask children to identify appropriate headings for different sections.

- Brainstorm key technical or subject-specific words. Ask children to help you spell and define them. Clearly display words and definitions for future use.

- Decide whether an annotated diagram is needed, and where it might appear.

- Stress that all texts need to end in a positive and interesting way if the reader is to remember them.

Group follow-up activities

You may decide that a variety of different topics is to be used for the children's independent texts.

red/blue/yellow   copymaster 16

Children plan their own non-chronological reports using the framework on copymaster 16. They can work in groups, in pairs or independently.

Guided group support

Red Help children plan clearly separated paragraphs of information and organise the paragraphs in a logical sequence with headings. Set a limit on the total number of paragraphs.

Blue As with the red group. Encourage the use of bullet points to organise sequence in paragraphs. Ensure that clear sub-headings are chosen, and help children see how these promote textual clarity.

Yellow Focus on the main body of the report and challenge children to extend the length of their text by planning a series of paragraphs dealing with different facts. Help them understand that, because the sections are discrete, a long report can be written without losing cohesion.

Plenary Volunteers show and discuss their plans. Discuss any concerns that have arisen during independent planning.

(5) Drafting the non-chronological report

Objectives To write clearly and concisely for a specific audience

To maintain an impersonal style

Shared session *You need: planning framework with notes from the previous session.*

*See **Drafting** on page 7 for more detailed advice on conducting a whole-class drafting session.*

- Follow the plan from the previous session, challenging children to compose their own formal impersonal sentences.

- Display and use as appropriate the list of key words children brainstormed in Session 4. Help children to understand that repetition of key words may be necessary for clarity, but encourage them to use pronouns when appropriate.

- Make sure appropriate headings are used, encouraging children to include key words. (Emphasise that section headings do not need to be full sentences.)

- Ask children to compose a closing sentence that will be memorable to the intended audience.

Group follow-up activities   **red/blue/yellow**

Children work on drafting their own texts.

Guided group support

Red Help children compose impersonal language. Make sure they do not feel threatened by it. If time allows, let them experiment with writing as if they were, for example, scientists. Encourage them to have fun using what they perceive to be the formal language of this profession.

Blue Ensure children stick to the plan and write their reports section by section. Remind children to focus on clarity, cohesion and impersonal style. Try out a few sentences for group discussion.

Yellow Challenge children to achieve full command of the formal style. Try out a few sentences for group discussion. Highlight and share appropriate examples of formal language. Highlight and discuss weaknesses.

Plenary   Volunteers read out sentences or paragraphs that they feel are successful. Others ask the class for help with sentences or paragraphs that are causing difficulty. Help steer discussions as necessary to keep children's writing on track for future sessions.

6 Revising and editing the non-chronological report

Objectives   To evaluate their own writing critically

To improve writing with a particular audience and purpose in mind

To record and acknowledge sources

Shared session   *You need: report draft (from Session 5), large sheets of paper.*

*See **Revising and editing** on page 7 for more detailed advice.*

■ Display the shared text that you drafted together in the previous session.

■ Recap on purpose and intended audience. Throughout this session, make explicit reference to the readership. For example, you might ask the children: *Do you think this would come over clearly to your audience?* or *How do you think this group of readers would cope with that word?*

■ Re-read the draft. Ask children to check that all the key information has been included and that all the key words have been used appropriately. Invite views on the level of formality in the text.

■ Make necessary revisions on the basis of children's feedback. Keep re-reading the text aloud so that children can hear improvements.

■ Direct children's attention to unclear or over-long sentences that they have not already spotted. Invite the class to improve them, giving suggestions for the children to evaluate.

■ If you have drawn information from a particular source or sources, show children how to acknowledge this under the heading 'Sources', listing the title (underlined) and author. Ask them to do the same for their own texts.

Group follow-up activities   **red/blue/yellow**

Children re-read their drafts and make revisions, either collaboratively or individually.

Guided group support

Red Focus on ensuring the text is clear and concise with appropriate use of pronouns and a good range of connectives. Encourage children to adapt text themselves. If necessary, offer alternatives.

Blue Help children to check that their report sounds clear, concise and impersonal, ensuring that all the necessary subject-specific vocabulary has been used. Direct them to weak areas and ask them to think of alternatives.

Yellow Focus on voice, style and vocabulary as with the blue group. Encourage children to check their own work. Challenge more able writers to extend their reports by adding information that was initially set aside. This might be presented in the form of explanatory text.

Plenary Encourage children to share successes and air concerns. Promote focused and helpful discussions that refer directly to the teaching objectives of the unit. Constantly bear in mind the intended audience for the text.

(7) Publishing the non-chronological report

Objectives To present the report in a form that is appropriate to the intended audience and purpose

If ICT is used, to discuss relevance of layout and font to the intended audience

Shared session *You need: report draft, sheets of A3 or A4 paper, different colour marker pens, ICT facilities (optional).*

*See **Publishing** on page 8 for more detailed notes on the issues involved in the final presentation of the text.*

■ Discuss how best to publish the report that you have written together. Relate your discussion to any points made at the planning stage. Bear in mind the needs and preferences of the audience.

■ If you have the necessary equipment, you may allow the children to present the class and/or individual reports using a desktop publishing system. If so, help them to use font and highlighting effects appropriately. More confident users of ICT could be encouraged to aim for more ambitious layouts.

■ Ensure that the children's work reaches its audience. For example, you might create an informative, interactive classroom display and invite another class to come and see it, or post it on the school's website and inform other classes that it is there.

Group follow-up activities **red/blue/yellow**

All children work towards the best possible presentation of their individual reports.

*Guided group support (**all groups**)* Help each child to focus on a manageable layout for their report, incorporating one or more annotated diagrams.

Plenary Invite to your classroom the intended audience for the report(s) that you have written. After they have read them, invite questions about how the reports were compiled. Encourage children in your class to respond. Then ask them to describe to the audience the key features of a non-chronological report and the principal stages involved in planning, composing, editing and refining it.

ADDITIONAL SESSION

 Writing up personal notes for others to read

Objectives

To revise note-making skills

To make effective notes that can be easily read and understood at a later date

To learn how to convert personal notes into notes for others to read

Shared session   *You need: OHT/poster 22.*

It would be helpful to do this session before the main unit on writing a report as children will need to make notes when writing their reports.

■ Display OHT/poster 22, masking the second activity (on expanding notes back into text). Remind children of the importance of making clear notes.

■ Ask children to help you cross out unnecessary words in the text until you are left with only key words and important information.

■ Together, write notes from the passage. Encourage children to use simple abbreviations or symbols where possible – for example, *Mars* need only be written in full at the beginning of the notes, thereafter it could be written simply as *M*. The children may remember & (*and*) and ∴ (*therefore*) from last term.

■ Your notes might begin something like this:

> Mars – nearest neighbour of Earth. M's surface often hidden by clouds of yellow dust. Rocky mountains orange and red due to rust – ∴ called 'red planet'.

■ Ask children if they think anyone could make sense of the notes. (Probably yes.)

■ If appropriate, show the children how these clear, coherent notes can be edited down even further by using word outlines (i.e. the most important consonants and initials) – for example, *mtns* for *mountains* or *pl* for *planet*).

■ Display the second text on the poster/OHT. Could anyone read these? (Probably not). Stress that notes such as these are fine as <u>personal</u> notes but are not intended for anyone else to read – even the person who made the notes would have to write them up quickly, before forgetting what they meant.

Group follow-up activities

1 red   pupil's book page 50

Children write out sentences in note form. They then compare their notes with a partner.

Guided group support Encourage children to add other abbreviations for common words. Help children find and highlight key words in the text. Give support in reducing the text as far as possible without losing meaning.

2 blue/yellow   pupil's book page 50

Children rewrite one of two short passages in note form. When they have finished, they swap notes with a partner who has worked on the other passage to try to reconstruct the original text. This is a good test of how clear the children's notes are.

Guided group support Make sure children use figures instead of words where numbers are used. Make sure that key words identified include relevant adjectives as well as nouns. Encourage children to think of abbreviations for the words that are most often repeated – for example, by using the initial letter only.

3 yellow   pupil's book page 51

Children condense their notes even further by experimenting with abbreviations and symbols.

Guided group support Help children experiment with reducing the longest words to 'word outlines' consisting of the most important consonants. Encourage them to invent abbreviations that might be useful for them in the future and could form part of their personal shorthand from now on. Stress that this must be consistent from one note-making session to the next, so that it becomes familiar.

Plenary   Children swap notes within their groups and try to read each other's work. Each group tells the class about any particular difficulties or successes.

 Homework suggestions

- Look at the contents page of an information text which you have recently used for research. Copy the main headings into the framework on copymaster 16, rearranging the order if you wish. Then make notes on the framework as if you were planning your own report. **(After Session 1)**

- Read a report and make notes on anything you find interesting. Comment on the style of writing, layout, use of headings, etc. Make a separate list of subject-specific words and their definitions.
  (After Session 2)

- Brainstorm a topic which you are currently working on. Write a list of key words and technical vocabulary. Using dictionaries and reference books, create a glossary giving clear definitions.
  (After Session 2)

- Watch a TV documentary about a subject that interests you. Listen to the commentary and identify similarities with written reports. Can you find any evidence of the three-part framework? Write down impersonal phrases that might be useful in your own report writing. Finally, talk to a friend about the differences between written and spoken reports.
  (After Session 3)

- Think of a subject you would like to know more about. Brainstorm and note everything you already know and decide what you would like to find out. Make a list of questions to research. Using books, CD-ROMs and/or the internet, make notes on the information you have found, and where you found it. **(After Session 3/Before Session 4)**

- Discuss with your family or friends a subject you know about, and might like to write about. Use the framework on copymaster 16 to plan the content of a report, including paragraph content and headings.

- Choose an information book, but do not open it. Use the title, cover illustrations and back cover blurb to predict the main sections listed on the contents page. Then predict the content of one section. Finally, open the book to find out how right you were!

- Make a list of ten key words related to a subject of your choice. Then look up these words in the index and/or contents pages of relevant books and CD-ROMs. Find out all you can about the words, noting your sources of information.

UNIT 4 — How to write a non-chronological report with explanation

Colour the right number of stars to show how well you did the following things:

0 stars = I didn't do it.   3 stars = I did it well.
1 star = I gave it a try.   4 stars = I did an excellent job!
2 stars = I did it quite well.

I adapted the framework for my own text.	☆	☆	☆	☆
I included some explanation.	☆	☆	☆	☆
I organised the information into clear paragraphs.	☆	☆	☆	☆
I used headings, sub-headings and bullet points.	☆	☆	☆	☆
I concluded my text with something interesting and useful.	☆	☆	☆	☆
I made good use of key words and technical vocabulary.	☆	☆	☆	☆
I wrote a glossary.	☆	☆	☆	☆
I wrote in a formal, impersonal style.	☆	☆	☆	☆
I acknowledged my sources.	☆	☆	☆	☆

Something I am especially pleased with

Something my audience liked in my writing

Something I'd like to do better next time

Term three fiction focus:
5 How to write a performance poem

What most children will already know:

That poetry is written in a variety of forms and for different audiences and purposes

That it is important to appeal to the target audience

How to write some different forms of poetry

How to create and use rhymes in poetry

That syllables in a line can be manipulated to produce a rhythmic effect

How to use other word-play effects

What children will learn in this unit:

To write in a particular voice and style

How to write a poem specifically for oral performance

How to redraft and polish work specifically for oral performance

How to manipulate stressed and unstressed syllables to create spoken rhythm

---

1 Analysing key features

Objectives

To recognise the key features of performance poetry

To evaluate a performance text for audience appeal

To identify the characteristics of Ogden Nash's work

Shared session

You need: OHTs/posters 23 and 24, copymaster 19, coloured pens, a large sheet of paper for class poster.

*A **zwieback** (OHT/poster 23, line 29) is a toasted sweet biscuit (from the German, meaning 'twice baked').*

- Tell children that they are going to write a poem to perform for an audience.

- Ask for examples of poems that are used mainly for performance (e.g. popular rap poems, or 'Custard the Dragon' by Ogden Nash, which features in **Cornerstones for Writing** Year 3, Term 3).

- What are the most important aspects of these poems? Briefly mention the 'three Rs' – **rhythm**, **rhyme** and **repetition**.

- Tell children you are going to read them 'The Adventures of Isabel' by Ogden Nash. Ask them to listen out for features that make it particularly enjoyable.

- Read the whole poem aloud in a lively way, emphasising the rhythm and using as much expression as possible. Ask children if they enjoyed it. What made it enjoyable to listen to? How did the author achieve this? Make sure you cover:
    - **Rhythm**: strong beat, easy to clap out, fast 'galloping' rhythm.
    - **Rhyme**: easy, repetitive rhyme scheme – simple pairs of rhyming lines (ensure children know these as **rhyming couplets**).
    - **Repetition**: repeated words and phrases; a repetitive chorus that may invite audience participation.
    - **Use of direct speech/dialogue**.
    - **Conversational style**: direct address to audience.
    - **Imagination**: unusual ideas and images, amazing events, use of strange, sometimes humorous, words and ideas.

Ogden Nash (1902–71)
Ogden Nash was an American poet and wit who was born in New York and studied at Harvard University. He published numerous volumes of witty and satirical light verse, characterised by unusual rhymes and puns. A sharply-focused observer, he often used his work to comment on the absurdities of life. While much of his poetry is funny, and often nonsensical, some of it contains a message.

- Display OHT/poster 23 (verses 1 to 3) and invite children to underline one or two examples of rhythm, rhyme and repetition, using three different coloured pens. Then ask them to underline/annotate other features using a fourth colour.

- Next, focus on Ogden Nash. Ask children what they know about him. If you wish, provide brief biographical details (see margin).

- Tell children you are going to re-read 'The Adventures of Isabel' and invite volunteers to join you. Help them to appreciate that performing a poem gives more life to the 'voice' of the poet than a silent reading.

- Elicit further observations regarding this particular poet's 'voice' and style. These may include:
  - surprise at finding such casual, conversational style in the work of a poet born at the beginning of the last century;
  - enjoyment of the fantasy element in his work.

- Explain that, when you go on to write your shared and individual texts, you will aim to replicate Ogden Nash's style.

Group follow-up activities

1 red   pupil's book page 52   (copymaster 19)

Children identify key features of 'The Adventures of Isabel' using the table in the pupil's book, which they copy out and fill in. (Alternatively, you could give children copymaster 19 and ask them to underline examples in the text.)

Guided group support Help children to check the poem against the key features table. Encourage close analysis and annotation of text. Ask them to try and find one further point of their own about how Ogden Nash writes, and why his work is enjoyable.

2 blue   pupil's book page 52   copymaster 20

Children use the table on copymaster 20 to identify key features of extracts from two performance poems, 'Jim' and 'The Charge of the Light Brigade'. Alternatively, you could give the group a blank OHT/poster and ask them to underline examples in the text in the pupil's book.

Guided group support As with the red group. Challenge the group to list elements of performance poetry that will be easy to reproduce and those that might be more difficult

3 yellow   pupil's book page 55   copymaster 20

Children use the table on copymaster 20 to identify key features in three extracts from performance poems. They then guess which one is by Ogden Nash. Alternatively, you could give the group a blank OHT/poster and ask them to underline examples in the text in the pupil's book.

Guided group support One of the three poems is by Ogden Nash. Children are asked to guess which. Challenge them to give reasons for their choice. ('The Song of Hiawatha' is by Henry Longfellow; 'Horatius', from 'The Lays of Ancient Rome', is by Thomas Macaulay; 'The Camel' is by Ogden Nash.)

Plenary

Invite all groups to feed back their findings and to compare and contrast. Identify common features and use this information to start a 'How to write a performance poem' poster.
Point out that, although 'The Adventures of Isabel' is a funny poem with a 'moral', performance poetry can also be serious. Ask for examples.
Recap on differences between performance poetry and other kinds of poetry as experienced by an audience. Cover the following points:
  - When hearing and/or seeing any performance, there is no time for personal reflection. The audience will react instantly to both the subject matter and the sound of the verse.

- When enjoying a poem privately, readers move through the text at their own speed and can reflect at length. Subtler meanings are discovered through readers' interpretation of figurative language and complex imagery.

If time permits, ask volunteers to read out the extracts from 'Jim' and 'The Charge of the Light Brigade' (pupil's book pp. 53–54).

(2) Analysing rhythm, rhyme and repetition

Objectives

To revise and identify rhythm and beat

To investigate syllabification and its contribution to beat and rhythm

To consider the pattern of stressed and unstressed syllables in a range of synonyms

To identify rhyme schemes

To identify repetition and alliteration

Shared session

You need: OHTs/posters 23, 24 and 25, copymaster 19, class poster (from Session 1).

Rhythm

■ Make sure children understand concept of **beat** (regular rhythm of stressed syllables – see Year 3, Term 3). Many poems with a strong beat contain the same number of stressed syllables in every line.

■ Display OHT/poster 23. Read verse 2 and ask children to clap the beat. How many beats are there in each line?

■ Select from verse 2 some lines that have a regular rhythm (e.g. lines 1 and 2). Ask a volunteer to read them aloud. Ask the same child to read quickly the last couplet (lines 9 and 10). He or she will probably have difficulty with the beat of line 10. Underline or circle the stressed syllables. Show that identifying these gives important clues as to how to perform the line:

> She <u>showed</u> no <u>rage</u>, she <u>showed</u> no <u>rancour</u>,
> But she <u>turned</u> the <u>witch</u> into <u>milk</u> and <u>drank</u> her.

■ Invite volunteers to mark on the OHT/poster the stressed syllables for the remaining lines of verse 2.

■ Invite children to read verse 1 aloud, with you clapping out the main stressed syllables (four beats per line).

■ Emphasise that the reader can bring out the beat in any poem by accentuating stressed syllables and 'packing' between them all unstressed syllables. Unstressed syllables also make an important contribution to rhythm. The more there are, the more of a tongue-twister the poem becomes. Why has Ogden Nash packed this poem so full of syllables? (To make it as lively as possible.)

■ Ask children to tap out each syllable quietly, using one finger against the palm of other hand, as you read verses 2 and 3 again. Choose a few lines and count the unstressed syllables in each. Help children to identify patterns. Try to agree on one or two. Express them as *de-dah-de-de*, etc.

■ Notice that there are often three syllables to a beat. That is what made verse 2, line 10 so difficult to read. Point out that verse 3, line 9, is also packed with unstressed syllables. Ask a volunteer to read it aloud and mark the stressed syllables on the OHT/poster. Does identifying them make it easier to read?

■ Allow children to experiment by elongating and exaggerating some stressed syllables and shortening those that follow. What effect does this have on the performance? (Makes it more exciting.)

■ Remind children that part of a poet's skill lies in choosing words that create an effective beat and rhythm. Encourage them to start thinking about this as they prepare to write their own poems.

Repetition

■ Focus again on verse 2, reminding the children about the 'three Rs'. Ask them to find and circle examples of repetition in verse 2 (e.g. *The witch's...* in lines 3 and 4; Isabel's name in lines 7 and 8).

■ Ask about the repetition of particular sounds in the verse – alliteration (e.g. *wicked witch* in line 2; *scream or scurry* in line 8).

Rhyme

■ Point out that another key element of writing in the style of Ogden Nash will be to replicate his witty rhymes.

■ Display OHT/poster 24 and read verse 4 aloud, telling children to listen out for rhymes. Ask children to help you underline each pair, using five different coloured pens. Emphasise that the rhymes are easily identifiable because they occur regularly at the ends of lines.

■ Repeat the process with verse 5. In what way is the rhyme scheme different? Notice the final, unpaired, line and talk about its effect (surprise, directness).

■ Display OHT/poster 25. Do children notice anything else about the rhymes in this poem? Ask for examples. Make sure you cover:

- Near-rhyme sometimes encourages reader to say words differently (*rancour/drank her*; *horrid/forehead*).
- Sometimes the same one-syllable word is used to end two lines (*you*; *up*; *off*).
- Unusual synonyms are sometimes chosen to create rhyme (*concoctor/doctor*; *ravenous/cavernous*).
- Sometimes a rhyme is made up of two words rather than just one (*drank her/rancour*; *fed off/head off*; *doctor/shocked her*).
- Normal word order may be manipulated to give an opportunity for unusual rhymes (*wrinkled/sprinkled*).

Group follow-up activities

1 red pupil's book page 57 copymaster 19

Children look at verses 1 and 3 of 'The Adventures of Isabel'. They underline the stressed syllables, use different coloured pens to mark the rhyme scheme and identify examples of repetition (include alliteration if appropriate).

Guided group support Ensure understanding of stressed and unstressed syllables. Encourage children to tap the desk quietly to emphasise stressed syllables and to tap their palms for unstressed syllables.

2 blue pupil's book page 57 (copymaster 21)

As activity 1, looking at the two poems children used in Session 1. They are also asked to look for examples of alliteration. Instead of using the copymaster, you could give each group a blank OHT/poster and ask them to underline examples from the text in the pupil's book.

Guided group support Focus on unstressed syllables and how they contribute to beat and rhythm. As children analyse the rhyme scheme, explain that matching pairs of rhymes are sometimes labelled with the same letter of the alphabet instead of the same colour.

3 yellow   pupil's book page 57   (copymaster 22)

As activity 2, looking at the three poems used in Session 1. Instead of using the copymaster, you could give each group a blank OHT/poster and ask them to underline examples from the text in the pupil's book.

Guided group support Focus on the effects of alliteration and repetition within each poem.

Plenary   Recap on the 'three Rs' – rhythm, rhyme and repetition. Write them up on the class poster, eliciting examples from each of the groups.
If time permits, ask for volunteers to read out performance poems from pages 54 to 56 of the pupil's book.

③ Identifying the structure

Objectives   To identify overall structure

To identify verse structure and create a framework for the children's own writing, based on a model text

Shared session   *You need: OHTs/posters 23 and 24, blank acetate.*

■ Recap on 'The Adventures of Isabel' and ask children to comment on the overall structure. How many verses are there? (five) How many lines in each verse? (usually ten) Explain that you are going to look at the structure of each verse in more detail.

■ Display OHT/poster 23 and ask children to listen as you read verse 1 aloud. Lay a blank acetate over OHT/poster 1 and elicit what happens in each couplet. Use different coloured pens to box and annotate each part of the text – for example:

> Lines 1 and 2: new character introduced
> Lines 3 and 4: new character described
> Lines 5 and 6: character speaks to Isabel, sets out problem
> Lines 7 and 8: reaction of main character
> Lines 9 and 10: how Isabel solves the problem

■ Remove your annotated acetate and lay it over another verse on OHT/poster 23. Go through each couplet in turn to check that the structure of the verse is the same. Help children recognise that the verses are structured in the same way.

■ What do they notice about lines 7 and 8? Stress that these two lines are exactly the same in every verse. What is the name for repeated lines such as these? (chorus)

■ Display OHT/poster 24 and lay the acetate over verse 4, showing that it follows the same pattern. Now lay it over verse 5 and ask children to comment on the structure (the first part of verse 5 follows the set structure, but it has been extended by seven lines).

■ Ask what is different about these lines. For example:

    ○ Narrative voice: the style of the poem changes from narrative (story-telling) to direct address. Ask children for examples of words that show this change (*Remember, Don't, look, say*). Point out the use of the imperative.

    ○ Punctuation: use of exclamation marks.

    ○ The last line is an 'odd' line that is not part of a couplet. It is shorter than all the others. What effect does it have? (Surprise!)

■ Ask children what the **purpose** of the last seven lines is? (To teach the reader a lesson: what to do in a frightening situation.)

■ Help children to analyse the subject matter. In verses 1 to 3, Isabel encounters a bear, a witch and a giant. Are these descriptions familiar? (Yes. They are similar to those found in well-known stories.) Is that why we enjoy them? Or is it that Isabel, with whom we can identify, calmly triumphs over each one?

■ Her fourth opponent (the doctor) is the most unusual and entertaining. Point out that he is a **caricature** (exaggerated for comic effect) of a familiar and trustworthy figure. Isabel's revenge fulfils the unspoken desire of many unappreciative patients. Children should be able to identify with this.

Group follow-up activities

1 red pupil's book page 58

Children work collaboratively to brainstorm lists of words to describe the appearance, actions, etc. of a selection of 'monsters' in the pupil's book. They then compose rhyming couplets about their chosen character(s).

Guided group support Challenge children to research unusual synonyms. Help them to use a thesaurus and/or rhyming dictionary.

2 blue pupil's book page 60

Children use a cloze-style verse framework to write an additional verse for 'The Adventures of Isabel'.

Guided group support Suggest that children try out ideas verbally and/or on whiteboards. Encourage use of a thesaurus and/or rhyming dictionary. Prompt children to choose unusual words and phrases.

3 yellow pupil's book page 61

Children write a list of real-life people who, though basically 'good', sometimes do things they may not like. They list key words about the personality/actions of each character, then generate entertaining rhyming couplets.

Guided group support Help children to identify other real-life characters who may have to be 'cruel to be kind'. Encourage them to create a caricature of one of these, exaggerating their most unpleasant characteristics.

Plenary Share and enjoy work from all groups. Encourage children to talk freely about any difficulties they have encountered. Make a class list of 'Helpful strategies' that children used to overcome them. Display it for future reference.

Discuss Isabel's final 'opponent', the nightmare. Help children to understand that there is a serious message here: counsellors often advise sufferers of nightmares either to learn to wake up or to challenge the *bugaboo* in their dreams. Talk about this 'human touch' as an aspect of Ogden Nash's work that should be incorporated into your writing project.

4 Planning the poem

Objectives
To use the writing framework constructed earlier

To replicate structural features and key content of a known text

To plan content in story form before attempting versification

Shared session
You need: framework sheet (OHT 23 with annotated acetate from Session 3).

■ Display the annotated framework from Session 3. Recap on the main points and remind children that its purpose is to help them write a poem in the style of Ogden Nash.

■ Tell children they are going to write a poem based on the structure of 'The Adventures of Isabel'. Decide together how many verses to write in the shared session (probably only one or two, and a final extended verse if appropriate).

■ Identify the audience for your shared text – if possible, a well-known audience from within school/community. Discuss its needs, likes and dislikes. Remind children that the purpose of the poem is to **entertain**.

■ Recap that it is helpful to plan content in prose. This will free children to concentrate on rhythm, rhyme, repetition, etc. when they are drafting the poem.

■ Choose a subject for your poem. Invent a hero/heroine – either a child or a community figure like a policeman or a shop-keeper. Agree on the character offering the best potential for a range of adventures.

■ Invent encounters that will test the character's bravery or ingenuity – one for each verse. Try to make each one markedly different. Challenge children to use their imagination to conjure up far-fetched adventures. Plan both description and action. Show that the problematic events arise directly from each opponent's 'bad' or scary nature. Decide on solutions that both suit the main character and resolve each problem.

■ Link content of the penultimate verse to a character whom children may wish to poke a little fun at – for example, a not-too-gentle dentist, a grumpy bus conductor.

■ Guide children in choosing a 'real-life issue' for the last verse – for example, how to deal with a bully or cheeky siblings. Help them think of a 'lesson' for last few lines.

Group follow-up activities
Discuss separate plans for children's independent work. Decide on audience (probably the same as for the shared work). Clarify whether children are to work alone, in pairs or groups.

red

Children concentrate on planning one more verse for 'The Adventures of Isabel', based on the framework in the pupil's book (p. 60).

Guided group support Focus this group firmly on content and basic structure. Encourage collaborative discussion to follow ideas through and ensure there is a clear solution to the problem.

blue

Children write one or two verses following the basic framework. If appropriate, include a caricature verse similar to verse 4 of 'The Adventures of Isabel'.

Guided group support Give assistance with planning detail, particularly as children plan the caricature verse.

yellow

Children produce their own fully developed version of the Ogden Nash poem.

Guided group support Challenge children to include a moral lesson in the last verse, following the model.

Plenary Volunteers describe their plans. Children compare notes on what has been hardest and easiest to do.
If time permits, ask children to predict what challenges drafting may bring.

(5) Drafting the poem

Objectives To compose verses of poetry according to a set structure

To use interesting and unusual synonyms

To manage rhyme within a set rhyme scheme

Shared session *You need: poem framework (from Session 4), thesaurus and/or rhyming dictionary.*

*See **Drafting** on page 7 for more detailed advice on conducting a whole-class drafting session.*

■ Recap on your previous planning session.

■ Help children to compose a fun chorus now, while levels of enthusiasm are high. Having this to build each verse around will enhance their enjoyment of the process.

■ Talk in detail about the main character and how he or she feels and behaves. Make notes and brainstorm a list of words. Decide on a key characteristic to form the basis of the chorus. Experiment with pairs of rhyming words that could be used to replicate Ogden Nash's chorus – for example:

> Aziz, Aziz didn't fluster,
> Aziz was too smart to bluster.

■ Where possible, challenge children to produce unusual expressions. For instance, the idea that a main character might be too calm to gnash her teeth could be translated into something much catchier:

> Mary didn't grind her choppers,
> She never exploded like party poppers.

■ Try out ideas and ask volunteers to perform some of the suggested choruses. Encourage other children to listen and guess how an audience might react. Invite a representative of the target audience to offer opinions.

■ Write each verse according to the plan. Focus children on writing rhyming couplets. Provide constant reminders of the process (*Now we need to...*).

■ Explore synonyms, using a thesaurus if necessary. Challenge children to find startling expressions and rhymes. Keep trying out different suggestions. Perform each couplet before adding it to the draft.

Group follow-up activities

red/blue/yellow

Children work on drafting their own texts.

Guided group support

Red Help children to compose a rhythmic and catchy chorus around which to base each verse. Focus them on creating coherent meaning as well as clever rhymes.

Blue Challenge children to use a wider range of vocabulary. Model/encourage use of thesauruses and rhyming dictionaries.

Yellow Encourage children to try out ideas for couplets by performing them, writing them on a whiteboard or scrap paper and then improving them before adding them to draft.

Plenary

Share and enjoy successful samples of work from volunteers. Encourage any children who are struggling to share drafting problems with their classmates.

6 Revising and editing the poem

Objectives

To check that original intentions have been carried out effectively

To experiment with adding, deleting and substituting words to achieve a polished final effect

To give priority to performance considerations when amending and improving text

To ensure that the written outcome is correctly spelled and punctuated

Shared session

You need: draft poems (from Session 5), coloured pens.

*See **Revising and editing** on page 7 for more detailed advice.*

- Congratulate children on the first draft. Explain that they are now going to improve it further.

- Emphasise that this is a 'script' for performance. Quality of sound must be children's first priority in considering revisions. Key areas for improvement will be those lines that do not sound as good as others. Ask children to focus on rhythm, rhyme and repetition as you read the draft aloud. Ask some children to clap the beat of stressed syllables. Invite others to tap the rhythm of unstressed syllables.

- Refer to the list of elements that made Ogden Nash's poem enjoyable (see p. 80). Have you included examples in your draft? Run through each in turn.

- Analyse problem lines, using a coloured pen to identify stressed syllables. Count them carefully. Change the number of syllables as necessary by deleting or inserting short words. Experiment with alternative words. Try changing the word order to create opportunities for insertion or deletion.

- Refer if necessary to any previous work on alliteration, onomatopoeia or other sound effects. If possible, include these to liven up the oral performance.

Group follow-up activities

red/blue/yellow

Children revise and edit their own texts. Encourage them to read their work aloud, preferably to classmates, and make any necessary adaptations.

Guided group support

Red Identify problem areas. Boost children's confidence by helping them with weaknesses in rhythm, rhyme, etc.

Blue Encourage children to collaborate by providing an audience for each other's work. Help them to identify strengths and weaknesses. Focus on ways to build in repetition.

Yellow Encourage children to listen to their own work from the point of view of an audience. Help them to incorporate alliteration and other word-play.

Plenary Try out a variety of amendments to selected couplets from the shared text – for example:

> The giant was hairy, the giant was horrid,
> He had one eye in the middle of his forehead.

This could have been written in a much less rhythmically interesting way as:

> The troll was tall, the troll was high,
> The troll had only got one eye.

Which do children prefer and why?
Volunteers give examples of ways they have improved their own texts. Invite other children to comment. Any child having difficulty in making improvements should be encouraged to ask for support from the class.

(7) Publishing/Performing the poem

Objectives To rehearse and perform work for a target audience

To compare and contrast a voiced rendition with a silent reading experience

Shared session *You need: final versions of children's poems.*

*See **Publishing** on page 8 for more detailed notes on the issues involved in the final presentation of the text.*

- Stress that the primary means of presenting performance poems to an audience is to perform them. Set a date for performing the poems within the school or community. Allow children time to rehearse. Show that you plan to make an occasion of the performance.

- Encourage children to perform their poems clearly and at an appropriate speed. Help them practise using their voices to bring out the beat and underlying rhythm whilst avoiding stilted rendition.

- Encourage children to add simple sound effects to enhance rhythm such as clapping or clicking to various rhythms and volumes. Choose one effect to accompany the main parts of each verse, with a contrasting effect for the chorus. Consider using musical instruments or sound effects to bring to life particular words or ideas.

- Suggest that children further illustrate poems with actions, varied facial expressions, hand gestures, etc.

- Point out that there will also be a written outcome. Help children present their poems neatly and attractively – perhaps as a word-processed book with illustrations, or as an attractive corridor display. Annotate to show sound effects and actions.

Group follow-up activities **red/blue/yellow**

Children rehearse their poems using sound effects and movements to entertain and help communicate meaning.

Guided group support (all groups) Provide an audience as children practise speaking and acting out their poems. Help them choose additional sounds that will accentuate beat and rhythm. Look for physical actions to help interpret meaning but encourage children to reject showy, meaningless routines. Note that less confident writers may particularly enjoy refining performance aspects.

Plenary Test first performances on classmates. Ask for positive criticism and build resulting changes into future rehearsals. Final dress rehearsals can later be brought back to the same audience to evaluate progress. Focus on celebrating and enjoying the children's work to boost their confidence before the final performance.

ADDITIONAL SESSIONS

Keeping a reading journal

See 'Keeping a reading journal' in Term 1, fiction focus (p. 39).

An additional copymaster (copymaster 23) is provided to help you vary the approach if you wish.

Writing from another character's point of view

Shared session *You need: OHT/poster 24, board/flipchart.*

- Explain to children that, though many pieces of writing have an **anonymous** narrator, they usually look at events through the eyes of one character only. Tell them that they are now going to learn to write from another character's viewpoint. To do this they will have to think about how this character behaves, and how he or she might feel.

- Ask children to think back to the poem 'The Adventures of Isabel'. Who is the narrator? Point out that, although the narrator remains anonymous throughout, the narrative is firmly focused on Isabel and her actions.

- Explain that, using evidence from the text, they are now going to imagine what the doctor might be like, and how he might have reacted to the events described. Tell them to think about words or phrases the doctor might use. What sort of voice might he have?

- Display OHT/poster 24 and read verse 4 of 'The Adventures of Isabel'. Ask the following questions and make notes of the children's ideas:
  - What adjectives might the doctor use to describe what happened when he visited Isabel? (*shocking, appalling, naughty, ungrateful, funny behaviour*)

- Why did the doctor come to visit? (We know from line 6 that Isabel was probably unwell. She might have had a tummy ache after all the strange things she had been eating [verses 1 to 3]. Perhaps her bad dreams [verse 5] had been keeping her awake.)

- Why did he *pinch and poke* Isabel? (He was checking to see what was wrong.) Did he mean to be unkind or to hurt her? (No – he wanted to help.)

- What do the children think the doctor gave Isabel when he said *Swallow this*? (Some pills from his satchel.)

- What do the children think happened when Isabel *cured the doctor*? Discuss lines 9 and 10. (She distracted his attention from his examination of her and took away the pills.) Have the children any ideas as to what she might have done with the pills? Might she have made the doctor swallow them instead? Or did she just surprise him so much that he did no more and went away? How might the doctor have reacted? What might he have said?

- How did the doctor feel when he left Isabel's house? (*angry, sick* [from taking the pills], *sad* [because Isabel wouldn't get better without them], *exasperated, amused*)

- What might happen next from the doctor's point of view? Does he have any plans for further action?

■ Make sure children understand that, by asking themselves similar questions, they can rewrite any text from another character's viewpoint.

Group follow-up activities

1 red pupil's book page 62

Children use a writing frame to write a letter from Isabel's doctor to his colleague, Dr Curall, describing his visit to her. What do they think Isabel's doctor's name might be?

Guided group support Ensure children consistently maintain the change to the first person retelling. Check for accurate use of pronouns and verbs.

2 blue pupil's book page 63

Children re-read the extract from 'Jim' and the lines describing what happened next. Using the writing frame on page 62, they write a letter from the lion's keeper to his boss, the Zoo Manager.

Guided group support Promote 'in role' retelling, encouraging children to explore personality by using special vocabulary. Challenge children to personalise the retelling as much as possible. Encourage them to make speculative additions.

3 yellow pupil's book page 63

Children compose and rehearse an oral description of the incident from the lion's point of view.

Guided group support Children do not need to refer to the letter framework on page 62, but might find useful prompts there to get them started. Ensure that they use a lively conversational style, noticeably different from the formal style of letter writing.

Plenary

Red and blue groups read their letters aloud. Yellow group performs oral retelling from the lion's point of view.
Ask the class to compare, contrast and evaluate all contributions.

Homework suggestions

- Choose a poem by a modern comic poet (e.g. Roger McGough, Michael Rosen, Spike Milligan). Compare and contrast it with a poem by Ogden Nash. Write in detail about similarities and differences. Say which you like better and why. Quote from both poems to justify your views. **(After Session 1)**

- Find a list poem, a narrative poem, a limerick, a haiku and a nonsense poem. Practise performing them. Record them on cassette and listen carefully to the replay. Which makes the best performance poem? Which is the worst? Give reasons for your choice. **(After Session 1)**

- Find a photograph or video of an animal. Brainstorm a list of words to describe its appearance, personality and behaviour. Use a thesaurus to find unusual synonyms. Find rhymes for these new words using a rhyming dictionary. Use pairs of rhyming words to write funny couplets about the animal. **(After Session 3)**

- Choose one of Ogden Nash's performance poems. Write/type it out and annotate it with performance notes. Use coloured pens to analyse rhythm. Decide how to use your voice. Make notes on actions or accompaniments. After the performance, ask your family and friends for feedback. **(After Session 7)**

- Make a collection of poems by different authors that you think would make good performance poetry. Write a description of sound effects and actions you would use with each. **(After Session 7)**

- Work with three friends. Choose a longer poem that you will all enjoy performing. Elect a **director** to decide who speaks when and how. Elect a **choreographer** to supervise hand/body movements and a **conductor** to advise on claps, clicks or use of instruments. Rehearse and perform the poem for your friends and family. **(After Session 7)**

UNIT **5** How to write a performance poem

Colour the right number of stars to show how well you did the following things:

0 stars = I didn't do it. 3 stars = I did it well.
1 star = I gave it a try. 4 stars = I did an excellent job!
2 stars = I did it quite well.

I made a detailed plan of verse structure and content.	☆	☆	☆	☆
I wrote unusual and entertaining rhyming couplets.	☆	☆	☆	☆
I achieved a good rhythm using stressed syllables.	☆	☆	☆	☆
I used repetition.	☆	☆	☆	☆
I used alliteration.	☆	☆	☆	☆
I wrote a chorus.	☆	☆	☆	☆
I made my work sound like Ogden Nash's voice and style.	☆	☆	☆	☆
I performed my poem with actions and sound effects.	☆	☆	☆	☆

Something I am especially pleased with

Something my audience liked in my writing

Something I'd like to do better next time

Term three non-fiction focus:
6 How to write a persuasive letter

What most children will already know:

How to distinguish between fact and opinion

How to identify persuasive writing

How to write a basic persuasive text

How to write in paragraphs

What children will learn in this unit:

How to organise a formal letter

How to construct an argument orally and in writing

How half-truth and bias can be used as persuasive devices

How opinions can be presented as facts

How to use persuasive language

How to link arguments together

 1 ## How to use persuasive devices

Objectives

To understand that opinion can be disguised as fact

To understand how half-truth is used as a persuasive device

To understand the concept of bias and how writing can be biased to support a point of view

Shared session

You need: OHTs/posters 26, 27 and 28 (plus copies of OHT/poster 28, for children to share in pairs), 3 different colour pens, large sheet of paper for class poster.

It would be helpful to do the Additional session on note-making and organising information (see p.105) before the main unit on writing a persuasive letter, as the children will need to use both these skills for their own letter writing.

■ Tell children they are going to learn how to write a persuasive letter to a newspaper.

■ Ask them what *persuasive* means (revising knowledge gained from Year 4, Term 3) and list their responses. Clarify the meaning of *to persuade* in the context of this unit (to cause another person to share your point of view about an issue). Tell children that there are several ways of doing this and you are going to investigate some of them in this session.

■ Tell children that a new pet shop, 'Ed's Exotic Pets', is due to open next week in the town of Rossington and that a lady called Mrs Cooper has written a letter to the local newspaper about it.

■ Read OHTs/posters 26 and 27 and ask children to think about why Mrs Cooper has written the letter (to protest against the opening of the pet shop and to persuade people that the exotic pet trade should be stopped). Do they think her letter will succeed?

■ Ask children the difference between **fact** and **opinion**. Write up definitions on a flipchart for children to refer to later.

■ Tell children that Mrs Cooper used a fact sheet about the exotic pet trade when she wrote her letter. Display and read OHT/poster 28. Explain that they are now going to find out how Mrs Cooper uses these facts to persuade her readers to adopt her point of view.

■ Display OHTs/posters 26 and 27 side by side and give pairs of children a copy of OHT/poster 28 to refer to. Explain that you are going to underline facts and opinions in different colours (write 'Fact' and 'Opinion' in these colours at the top of the OHT/poster).

■ Begin by asking the children to identify any straightforward facts which Mrs Cooper has used (e.g. the lizard and python; the RSPCA finding animals abandoned).

■ Next, ask children to identify pure opinions in the letter. Look at the statements in the first paragraph and ask whether these are facts or opinions. Discuss why Mrs Cooper does not write these in the first person – for example, *I believe that...* (she is presenting her personal opinions as facts). Explain that in persuasive writing opinions are often presented as facts.

■ Mrs Cooper also **manipulates** some facts by inserting words that reflect her own opinion and then presenting them as statements of truth. Ask children to look for examples of this (e.g. *exotic animals are <u>cruelly</u> captured*; Mrs Cooper's belief that the animals' crates are too small).

■ Tell children that another way to manipulate facts is to turn them into **half-truths**. Can children suggest what this might mean? (A statement that deliberately tells only part of the truth or exaggerates a fact.) Write 'Half-truth' on OHT/poster 26 in a third colour and write a definition on the flipchart. Ask children to find examples (e.g. 51% is only <u>just</u> *more than half*; the number of convicted pet shop owners and staff <u>has</u> doubled but the actual numbers are relatively small – both half-truths give an exaggerated impression of the truth by withholding statistics). Can children suggest an even more exaggerated way of expressing *more than half*? (e.g. *most*)

■ Write the word **bias** on the flipchart and ask children to suggest a definition. Do they think that Mrs Cooper's letter is biased? To help, ask whether she mentions any advantages of selling or owning exotic pets, or anything about exotic pets being well cared for (there is only one line: *Naturally, some owners are capable...*). Does she use <u>all</u> the facts from the factsheet? Which has she missed out, and why?

■ Explain that these are all devices people use when trying to persuade someone to adopt their opinion. Tell children that they are now going to practise some of these themselves.

Group follow-up activities

1 red   pupil's book page 64

Children read sentences and classify them as facts or opinions.

Guided group support Encourage children to discuss the differences between facts and opinions and to justify their choices.

2 red   pupil's book page 65

Children write two captions for each photo, from two opposing points of view.

Guided group support Work with children to verbalise their captions before writing them. Ask them to explain why their caption reflects a certain point of view.

3 blue/yellow   pupil's book page 66

Children read the extract from a newspaper report on exotic pets and rewrite it as a biased piece.

Guided group support Encourage children to select information, write opinions as facts and use half-truth. Compare completed pieces of writing that reflect opposing points of view.

Plenary Make a poster entitled 'How to write a persuasive letter'. Ask children what they have learnt so far about how to write persuasively. Write up their responses and use this as an opportunity to reinforce the main objectives of the session (the use of bias, half-truth and opinions presented as facts). Ask children to read some of their work while the others identify which persuasive devices have been used.

② Investigating the style of a persuasive letter

Objectives To understand the style of a persuasive letter

To investigate the use of persuasive language

To collect words and phrases which will be useful when writing a persuasive letter

Shared session *You need: OHTs/posters 26 and 27, large sheet of paper, class poster (from Session 1).*

■ Tell children they are going to find out about persuasive writing techniques and to collect some words and phrases that will be useful when they write their own persuasive letter.

■ Create a class chart entitled 'Useful persuasive words and phrases'.

■ Re-read the letter on OHTs/posters 26 and 27. Ask children to identify and underline any words or phrases which Mrs Cooper uses to make her writing more persuasive. Write these up on the class chart.

■ Underline *Surely* (in para. 3). Ask children why this word is persuasive (it assumes that there could be no other reasonable point of view). Write the word on the chart.

■ Underline *Naturally, some owners are capable of looking after exotic animals. However, many...* (para. 4). Ask children why this is persuasive. (By acknowledging another viewpoint, Mrs Cooper makes her argument appear balanced, based on a knowledge of the facts on both sides. However, she uses the words *some* and *many* without giving supporting evidence or statistics.) Write the phrases *Naturally, some...*, *However, many...* on the chart.

■ Underline the question *If this happens, what is to become of these animals?* (para. 4) and ask children whether they think Mrs Cooper expects a direct answer. Why is this question persuasive? (It <u>suggests</u> that terrible things happen to the animals.) Do children know what this sort of question is called? Add **rhetorical questions** to the chart.

■ Can children suggest any other words or phrases which could be substituted for *Naturally, some...* (e.g. *Of course..., Lots of people are..., Indeed..., There are many people who...*)? Write some of their suggestions on the chart and then substitute them orally into the letter, reading the text back for meaning. Reinforce the point that acknowledging the opposite point of view can be a useful persuasive tool.

■ Ask children to suggest some other rhetorical questions and where these might fit into the letter. Read the text back, including these questions, and discuss their effectiveness.

■ Finally, underline the words *Furthermore* (para. 3), *Consequently* (para. 4) and *Therefore* (para. 5) and discuss their meanings. Re-read the sentences to the children, first omitting the words, then including them. Ask children which they think sounds better and why. Explain that these words are useful when writing a persuasive letter as they link the argument together. Write them on the class chart under the heading 'Linking words'.

Group follow-up activities

 1 red   pupil's book page 67   copymaster 24

George is trying to persuade Mum to allow him to keep a snake. Children act out the scenes orally in pairs, taking turns to play George. They then write the argument in the speech bubbles.

Guided group support Help children to understand that there are two sides to an argument. Encourage them to use the persuasive language from the chart.

 2 blue/yellow   pupil's book page 67

Children read the transcript of an interview for a news bulletin. They work as a group to distinguish and list the persuasive words and linking words.

 3 blue   pupil's book page 68   copymaster 25

Children fill in the blanks on the copymaster with persuasive and linking words. As an extension, they can add some of their own arguments orally or in writing. Finally, the group can decide which team the fan supports!

Guided group support Help children to identify the persuasive and linking words. Complete the cloze procedure orally first to reinforce the correct use of the vocabulary in context.

 4 yellow   pupil's book page 68

Children use the persuasive vocabulary to prepare orally another bulletin, giving the opposite point of view. This can be recorded on to a cassette or written and presented.

Guided group support Help children to select the persuasive and linking vocabulary. Encourage them to use the vocabulary in the correct context in their oral work.

Plenary

Ask children what they have learnt about using persuasive language.
Write their responses on the class poster which you started in Session 1. Ensure that children have understood the use of rhetorical questions, and the importance of acknowledging the opposite point of view.
Next, compile a 'Useful persuasive words and phrases' chart. Ask children to contribute words from their group work. Encourage the red group to contribute to this by asking them what they have written in their speech bubbles.

3 How to organise a persuasive letter

Objectives

To learn the layout of a formal letter

To understand the purpose of each section of the letter.

Shared session

You need: OHTs/posters 26 and 27, 5 different colour pens.

 Tell children you are going to learn how to organise a formal letter. Ask children to distinguish between a formal and an informal letter, and to suggest when each might be used.

*The children could also be told that if the recipient's name is known, then the closure is **Yours sincerely**.*

■ Return to OHTs/posters 26 and 27. Draw a box round *Dear Sir/Madam* and label it 'Greeting' or 'Salutation'. Tell children that this is a formal greeting that is used when the recipient's name is unknown.

■ Draw a box round *Yours faithfully* and label it 'Closure'. Ask children why the letter does not end with *Love from... or See you soon...* Emphasise that this is the way to end a formal letter that begins *Dear Sir/Madam*.

■ Ask children to locate the two addresses on the letter. Draw boxes round them in different colours. Label them 'Sender's address' and 'Receiver's address'. Emphasise that the receiver's address is only used on a formal letter.

■ Next, look at the main body of the letter. Tell children that there are three main parts to the structure of the text. Use different colours to box paragraph 1, paragraphs 2, 3, and 4, and finally paragraph 5. Tell children they are going to investigate what 'job' each part of the letter does.

■ Re-read paragraph 1. Discuss the content of this paragraph with the children. The writer clearly states her position on the issue. Underline *I am writing to...* Label the box 'Introduction (state position)'.

■ Next, discuss and label the second box. This is the main section of the letter. Label it 'Main section (argument)'. Tell children that you will return to look at it in more detail later.

■ Discuss and label the last box. This is the conclusion. It contains a summary of the arguments, and asks for some action to be taken. Label the box 'Conclusion (summary and action)'.

■ Return to the second box. Note that this section is divided into short paragraphs. Draw a box round each paragraph. Discuss the content of the first paragraph and label the box 'Argument 1: Capturing exotic animals'. Point out that the paragraph begins by making a point, which is then supported by **evidence**.

■ Repeat this for paragraph 3 (Argument 2: Pet shops) and paragraph 4 (Argument 3: Looking after exotic animals). Ask children why the arguments have been presented in this order. Discuss the logical steps of the argument: capturing animals → selling animals → keeping animals.

Group follow-up activities

1 red   pupil's book page 69   copymaster 26

Children read a letter in support of keeping exotic pets. They draw boxes around each section and label them, inserting the correct greeting and closure and writing their own address.

Guided group support Discuss the structure of the letter and how to write an address.

2 blue   pupil's book page 69   copymaster 27

Children cut up the jumbled version of a persuasive letter on the copymaster. They work in pairs to re-organise the letter correctly.

Guided group support Discuss the structure of the letter and how the middle section is organised to form a logical argument.

3 yellow   pupil's book page 69

Children read the mixed-up middle section of a letter in support of keeping exotic pets. They re-organise the main points of the middle section and write the opening and concluding paragraphs, using appropriate language and argumentative techniques learnt from Sessions 1 and 2.

Guided group support Help children to choose appropriate vocabulary for the opening and concluding paragraphs.

Plenary   Return to the class poster, 'How to write a persuasive letter'. Ask children what they have learnt about organising a formal persuasive letter. Write up their responses. Make sure that the key teaching points are reinforced here (formal greeting and closure, use of paragraphs to order the argument logically).

4   How to construct and present an argument

Objectives   To construct an argument and persuade others of your point of view

To present the argument orally

To evaluate the effectiveness of the arguments

Shared session   *You need: OHT/poster 29, a large sheet of paper.*

1 This session is linked to the Additional session on note-making and provides an opportunity for children to make use of their research.

2 Children will present their point of view orally to the group/class before they write it as a letter. Presenting the argument orally before writing will give children practice in using the persuasive devices and language that they have learnt in Sessions 1 and 2. It will allow them to organise an argument and verbalise their thoughts before they write. Speaking and listening is an essential step when using new, unfamiliar language.

3 Children are more likely to write well when the subject is something that directly concerns and interests them. Therefore, you may prefer to base the following sessions on a subject decided upon with the children. (See 'Alternative group activities' at the end of this session.)

■ Tell children they are going to pretend they have been invited to a talk show on local radio to present their point of view on the issue of circus animals.

■ Divide the class in two: half to argue <u>for</u> and half <u>against</u> the issue. Children work in pairs to think of evidence to support their point of view (based on their research from the Additional session and/or their own ideas).

■ Tell children that they are now going to look at some more evidence that they could use to support their arguments. Display and read OHT/poster 29.

■ Create two columns on a flipchart/large sheet of paper, 'For' and 'Against' and work with the children to split the evidence under these headings. Choose one side of the argument first and note the evidence from OHT/poster 29 which clearly supports it. Discuss whether there is any evidence which needs to be left out as it does not support that point of view. Then remind children of the word **bias** and the work they did in Session 1. Can any of the evidence be manipulated (e.g. by adding words) or are there any half-truths that could be used?

■ Tell children that they need to make notes to remind them of their main points when they are being interviewed on the radio. Ask children to identify four main points. Write these together, in note form, on the flipchart. (Save these for the next session.) Emphasise that these notes are a personal reminder for the interviewee. (Preparing interview notes will help children to plan their letters in the next session.)

■ Interview notes for speaking <u>against</u> performing animals might look like this:

Purpose:	tell everyone about cruelty of performing animals in circuses
Main points:	animals captured from wild
	not enough space for animals – not like natural habitat
	cruelty of owners – training
	people can see animals on TV
Conclusion:	performing animals banned – human circuses only

■ Present the argument orally, using the notes for support and demonstrating the use of persuasive language. You could record this as a 'pilot' radio interview with one child acting as the radio interviewer. Children then comment on whether the argument was/wasn't effective in persuading them to adopt the interviewee's point of view.

Group follow-up activities

All groups will need a large piece of paper.
Tape recorders would also be useful to record the children's group work, especially as some may not wish to present their work to the class.

1 red pupil's book page 70

Children use the information on page 70 (and pp. 72–73 if they have completed the first additional session or if you feel the group can handle this extra information). They organise the points into the given categories and present their case to the group. If you wish to provide extra scaffolding, give children some ready-prepared interview notes to allow them to concentrate on their oral presentation.

Guided group support Work with children to select information to support their argument. Encourage them to use persuasive language in their presentation.

2 blue/yellow pupil's book page 71

Children use the information on page 71. They decide whether they are 'For' or 'Against' performing animals. They select the relevant information and add their own. You could give them some categories to help them organise their information (e.g. training, living conditions). They make notes and present their case to the group.

Guided group support

Blue Work with children to select and analyse information to support their argument. Encourage them to write short 'prompt' notes and to use persuasive language in their presentation.

Yellow As with the blue group. Ask children to consider the most effective way of organising their argument.

3 red/blue/yellow pupil's book page 71

Children take it in turns to present their case to the rest of the group. They then decide on a representative to present their case in the plenary.

Plenary

A member of each group is 'interviewed' for the radio and presents their case to the class. After each presentation, children are asked about the effectiveness of the argument. If both sides of an issue have been presented, a vote could be taken. It is useful if the presentations are recorded. They can then be played back to illustrate key points about structure or use of persuasive devices or language.

Finally, ask children what they have learnt about constructing an argument. Reinforce key points and write these on the class poster 'How to write a persuasive letter'. The children should now have a list of 'rules' for the writing that they have investigated themselves, as well as a list of useful vocabulary to use when writing.

Alternative group activities

You could adapt the notes given above to focus on an issue decided upon with the children. The issue will need to be contentious enough to enable children to create an effective argument, for example:

- issues concerning school (e.g. uniform, tuck shops, school dinners, improvements to the school environment);
- the local area (e.g. new facilities – park/youth club, litter);
- global issues (e.g. hunting, animal testing, conservation).

Children will need some knowledge of the subject to support their point of view. This will involve researching the topic to collect facts, or conducting research in school or the local area. Children could use books and the internet, carry out observations, surveys and interviews. They could also write to organisations, requesting information concerning their issue. This research could be undertaken in other lessons, then used in the Literacy Hour. Alternatively, a literacy lesson could be used <u>before</u> this step to allow children to research their topic. (See the Additional session on note-making and organising information.)

5 Planning the letter

Objectives
To plan a formal persuasive letter in note form

To select relevant information

To organise arguments

Shared session
You need: copymaster 28, class poster, interview notes from Session 4.

■ Tell children they are going to write a letter about the issue of circus animals. Establish the purpose of and audience for your letters. Write the purpose on the board and discuss which newspaper you should send your letters to. The children could send their letters to a children's newspaper (see list of useful addresses on p. 104).

■ Write up on the board/flipchart the framework given on copymaster 28.

■ Start the letter by writing in the address boxes: label these 'sender's address' and 'receiver's address'.

■ Write the greeting *Dear Sir/Madam*, then the closure *Yours faithfully*.

■ Tell children that you are going to start by planning the main body of the letter in note form. Recap on what the different paragraphs should contain and write the following planning guidelines on the board/flipchart (save this for the next session):

> **paragraph 1:** state purpose and position
> **middle paragraphs:** arguments (give each paragraph a heading to make the main argument clear; write notes for the supporting evidence)
> **final paragraph:** re-state the position and note what action should be taken

■ Display the interview notes from Session 4 and explain that you will use these to help you. A plan for the middle section of a letter arguing against performing animals might look like this:

> Para.1: **Purpose and position**
> protest – performing animals – circuses
> cruel – should be stopped
>
> Para. 2: **Capture**
> captured – wild
> baby elephants – mother shot
>
> Para. 3: **Transport**
> transported – terrible conditions
> containers too small – lion cub paralysed
>
> Para. 4: **Training**
> cruel training methods
> bears – burn paws
> tigers – beaten
>
> Para. 5: **Summary and action**
> all performing animals banned
> boycott animal circuses
> letters to local council – ban on circuses in area
> sign petition

■ Tell children they are now going to plan their own letters in note form.

Group follow-up activities

1 red   copymaster 28

Children use the copymaster to plan their letter in note form, using their notes from Session 4.

Guided group support Work on planning in note form, making sure that children understand the notes and can follow the plan.

2 blue

Children copy the framework from the board/flipchart into their book and use it to plan their letter in note form, using their notes from Session 4.

Guided group support Work with children on planning in note form and on organising their arguments.

3 yellow

Children use their notes from Session 4 and write the plan for their letter into their books.

Guided group support Work with children on planning in note form and on writing an organised middle section which contains more than three main arguments.

Plenary

Ask children what they have learnt about planning the letter.
Address any problems experienced at the planning stage – for example, organisation/repetition of points, using longhand instead of notes.
Use one of the children's plans (with permission) to demonstrate how such problems might be solved.

6 Drafting the letter

Objectives

To write a persuasive letter, following a plan

To include persuasive words and phrases

To link paragraphs together

To use bias and half-truth and present opinion as fact

Shared session

You need: class poster, useful word chart, letter plan (from Session 5), flipchart, 5 different colour pens.

 *See **Drafting** on page 7 for more detailed advice on conducting a whole-class drafting session.*

■ Tell children you are going to draft the letter to the newspaper.

■ Display your 'How to write a persuasive letter' poster and remind children about the persuasive devices which can be used. Reinforce their understanding of bias, half-truth and how to disguise opinion as fact.

■ Display the 'Useful words and phrases' chart. Remind children about the persuasive phrases and the linking words that are used when writing a persuasive letter.

■ Display these charts alongside the letter plan as you write.

■ Write the letter together, constantly re-reading and changing words and phrases as necessary. You will need to remain in firm control of the writing, while asking children for their contributions. Explicit references to the use of persuasive language and phrases should be made throughout the shared writing.

■ You could use different colours for different sections of the writing to emphasise the structure. This is especially useful in the middle section of the letter.

■ Finally, read the complete letter through with the children. Remind them that this is only a first draft and that further modifications may need to be made at the revising and editing stage.

■ Tell children that they are now going to draft their own letters.

Group follow-up activities

red

Children draft their letters, following their plans. Support may be given by drafting the initial paragraph as a group, or by giving children copies of the framework on copymaster 28. Additional support may be given by providing the first sentence of each paragraph on the framework.

Guided group support Work with children on following a writing plan. Encourage them to use persuasive language and some linking words in their writing.

blue/yellow

Children draft their letters, following their plans.

Guided group support

Blue Encourage children to use persuasive language and help them to link paragraphs.

Yellow Encourage children to include half-truth and to present opinion as fact.

Plenary Ask children if they have experienced any difficulties when drafting the letter. Alternatively, use points which have arisen during the guided sessions. Use the plenary session to reflect on these difficulties and to revise key points.

 Revising and editing the letter

Objectives To assess the effectiveness of the letter

To improve the letter by revising

Shared session *You need: class letter draft, large sheets of paper.*

*See **Revising and editing** on page 7 for more detailed advice.*

■ Tell children that they are going to revise their letters. Model this using the class letter.

■ Choose one or more of the following revision focuses:
- organisation;
- writing opinions as facts;
- using half-truth;
- using persuasive words and phrases;
- using linking words.

■ You might choose something that several of the children have had difficulties with or an issue which has arisen in the plenary sessions or when marking the draft letters. Write the revision focus at the top of the sheet.

■ Discuss possible changes with the children and alter the text accordingly, using a different colour.

- Children then revise their own letters. They will need to be given a revision focus.

- You may wish to correct other errors which are not part of the revision focus, or to spend another session proof-reading for spelling and punctuation errors.

Group follow-up activities

red/blue/yellow

Children work on revising their own letters.

Guided group support

Red Work with children to check that their arguments make sense and that they have used some persuasive words and phrases.

Blue Work with children to check that they have used persuasive and linking words and phrases in the correct context.

Yellow Ask children to identify where they have used half-truth or disguised opinion as fact, and discuss any further opportunities for this. Encourage them to use persuasive and linking words and phrases.

Plenary Children feed back on their revising and editing work. They report on what they have learnt and how this will help them when they write letters in the future. Ask children for examples of something which they have changed, and how this has improved their letter in relation to the revision focus.

⑧ Presenting and sending the letter

Objectives To present a letter

To address an envelope correctly

Shared session *You need: class letter draft, writing paper, envelopes.*

1 See **Publishing** on page 8 for more detailed notes on the issues involved in the final presentation of the text.

2 A4 paper with a line guide underneath looks more 'official' than lined A4 paper.

- Tell children that they are going to present their letters, address the envelopes and send them to the newspaper.

- Using the class letter, model writing an address.

Here are some useful addresses:

The Newspaper,	Enquiries Service,	Chester Zoo,
P.O. Box 121	RSPCA,	Chester,
Tonbridge,	Causeway,	Cheshire
Kent	Horsham,	CH12 1LH
TN12 5ZR	W. Sussex	
www.thenewspaper.org.uk	RH12 1HG	

This is a children's newspaper. It has lots of good articles and publishes children's letters on issues that concern them.

- Tell children that they will need to estimate the space needed for the sender's address by looking at the longest line and deciding where to begin writing.

- Next, model writing the receiver's address and the greeting, explaining aloud exactly what you are doing as you write.

- Secure the children's understanding of the layout of paragraphs and how to end the letter.

- Finally, model the addressing of the envelope. Point out that it is the same as the recipient's address on the letter.

- The children are now ready to present their own letters and to address the envelopes.

- Give each child a piece of paper and an envelope. Children address an envelope for their letter. These can then be placed in a large envelope to send to the newspaper.

Group follow-up activities **red**

Children present their letters and address envelopes. Support may be given by shared writing the address for the envelope with children first.

Guided group support Work with children to ensure that the letters are presented clearly.

yellow/blue

Children present their letters and address envelopes.

Guided group support Work with children on clear presentation of the letter and the address.

Plenary Review the letters, post them (with the children if possible) and wait for a reply!

ADDITIONAL SESSIONS

How to make notes and organise information

Objectives To skim and scan for relevant information

To make notes

To organise notes

Shared session *You need: OHTs/posters 30 and 31, a large sheet of paper.*

It would be helpful if this session were done before the main unit on writing a persuasive letter, as the children will need to make notes and organise information for their own letter writing.

- Tell children that they are going to learn how to make notes from different sources and organise them.

- Tell them that a lady called Mrs Cooper is writing a letter to the newspaper to protest against the opening of an exotic pet shop in her area. She believes that the pet shop should not be opened, but she needs some facts and information to support her view. She has found some information, but she now needs to make notes and work on organising it.

- Read the information on OHTs/posters 30 and 31 to the children. Discuss why Mrs Cooper used the internet to find her information.

- Remind children about the purpose of note-making. Work with them to put a bracket around the sections of the text which they think would be most useful to Mrs Cooper. Concentrate on factual information (rather than opinion), quotations or ideas for campaigns.

■ Revise how to make notes by underlining key words and missing out words which are not important. Write the key words – for example:

> Lizard – starving to death – Leeds shop

> RSPCA – animals found in streets – Burmese python, turtle, iguanas, bearded dragons

■ Look at the notes and ask children what needs to be done with them to make them more useful to Mrs Cooper when she is writing her letter (they need to be **organised** in some way).

■ Discuss how the notes could be categorised, for example under headings: 'Capture', 'Transport', 'Pet shops', 'Owners'.

■ Organise the information under these headings. (Some information may be relevant to more than one heading. Children will have to decide which argument the information best supports.)

■ Tell children that they are now going to make notes and organise information in the same way.

Group follow-up activities

1 red   pupil's book page 72

Children read the information on page 72 and write down key words under given headings. They then use the notes to construct complete sentences.

Guided group support Discuss which words are the most important and help the children categorise the information. Encourage them to verbalise a sentence from their notes before writing it down.

2 blue   pupil's book page 72

Children read the information on page 73 and make notes, organising them into the given categories. You can provide further scaffolding by telling children which paragraphs to make notes from, thereby 'filleting' the relevant information.

Guided group support Ask children to skim-read the text first to get an overview of the main points. Help them to organise their notes into the given categories, encouraging them to use different or sub-categories if they need to.

3 yellow   pupil's book page 72

Children read the information on page 73 and decide what is relevant. They make notes, organising them into sections.

Guided group support Ask children to read the texts first and decide how to categorise the information. Help them to select the most important information, make notes and organise them into categories.

Plenary Ask children what they have learnt about making notes and organising information. Discuss the information they have read, and how they categorised it. Ask how they think this is going to help them when they write their letters to the newspaper. Stress that it will give them **evidence** to support their point of view.

Alternative group activity

This is particularly suitable for use <u>after</u> the main unit.

Children research their own topic, make notes and rewrite information in their own words. This is a good opportunity for children to carry out research for their own letters from information leaflets, books, newspapers, the internet, etc. The activity provides a <u>purpose</u> for their research.

How to write a persuasive leaflet

Objectives
To use persuasive language

To set out an argument clearly using bullet points

To understand that pictures can be persuasive

Shared session *You need: OHT/poster 32, OHTs/posters 26 and 27 (optional).*

This session is best tackled after the main unit. It provides a good contrast of style to the persuasive letter.

■ Tell children they are going to learn how to write a **leaflet**. Ask them whether they know what a leaflet is. If possible, show them some examples of leaflets including the ones they may have brought in from home (see Homework suggestions). Ask them to identify the purpose of the leaflets.

■ Display OHT/poster 32. Tell children that this is a leaflet which has been distributed to all the houses in the town of Rossington. Read the leaflet together.

■ Clarify that the **purpose** of the leaflet is to protest against the opening of the pet shop.

■ Ask children if they think the leaflet is effective. (Comparisons may be drawn between the effectiveness of Mrs Cooper's letter on OHTs/posters 26 and 27 and this leaflet – both were written for the same purpose.)

■ Ask children what they noticed first about the leaflet. Underline words in large type and discuss <u>why</u> these words have been made to stand out (they convey the message clearly and simply, and catch the reader's attention). The message is like a **headline** or a **slogan**, using **alliteration** and **direct language**.

■ Next, look at the pictures and discuss why these are persuasive (they imply that the animals are badly treated and that the town of Rossington will be in danger from escaped snakes). Ask what the effect would be if the writer had chosen a picture of a turtle in a large tank with rocks and a sun-lamp to bask under. Emphasise that pictures can be used as powerfully as words.

■ Look at the way the arguments have been set out in the middle section of the leaflet.

■ Introduce the term **bullet points** and write it on the leaflet. Ask why the writer has chosen to set his/her argument out in this way (bullet points enable the reader to get the information quickly and easily, and the purpose of the leaflet is to give information quickly, in an accessible format). Emphasise that the information is still organised in a logical way, with the points about capture first, then transport, etc.

■ Tell children that they are now going to write their own leaflets.

Group follow-up activities
Children can either write a leaflet relating to the issue they chose and researched (if you followed the alternative option in Session 4 and/or the Additional session) or do the activities given in the pupil's book.

1 red   pupil's book page 74
Children write a leaflet in support of 'Ed's Exotic Pets', using given arguments. They write a 'catchy' heading for the leaflet and think about pictures to support their argument (they can draw these, if time permits).

Guided group support Work with the children to write 'catchy' headings and discuss which one is best and why. Help them to think about what kinds of illustration might persuade the reader to adopt their point of view.

2 yellow/blue   pupil's book page 74

Children design a leaflet in support of 'Ed's Exotic Pets'.

Guided group support Encourage children to write a 'catchy' heading and to organise their arguments using bullet points. Help them to think about persuasive illustrations.

Plenary   Ask children what they have learnt about writing a leaflet. Emphasise the main objectives of the lesson.

Ask several children to share their leaflets, while the others decide which ones are effective and why.

Homework suggestions

- Look for examples of half-truth, bias and fact presented as opinion in newspapers, magazines, leaflets, etc. Then find examples of these things on television and radio and make notes of what you discover. **(After Session 1)**

- Look for examples of persuasive and linking language in newspapers and magazines. Make a list of these words to add to your class word bank. **(After Session 2)**

- Look in newspapers or magazines for letters which put forward a point of view. Investigate the structure of these letters, looking for arguments supported by evidence. **(After Session 3)**

- Write down your own address, including the postcode. **(After Session 3)**

- Listen to radio or television interviews with people putting forward their point of view (e.g. 'Newsround' or radio news programmes). **(After Session 4)**

- Interview your friends and family about an issue. Make notes. **(After Session 4)**

- Find information about a chosen issue from different media sources or by conducting surveys/interviews, etc. **(After 'How to make notes and organise information')**

- Find some leaflets and analyse their purpose. **(After 'How to write a persuasive leaflet')**

UNIT 6 How to write a persuasive letter

Colour the right number of stars to show how well you did the following things:

0 stars = I didn't do it.   3 stars = I did it well.
1 star = I gave it a try.   4 stars = I did an excellent job!
2 stars = I did it quite well.

I wrote addresses correctly.	☆	☆	☆	☆
I used the correct greeting and closure for a formal letter.	☆	☆	☆	☆
I organised my arguments well.	☆	☆	☆	☆
I used evidence to support my arguments.	☆	☆	☆	☆
I linked my paragraphs together.	☆	☆	☆	☆
I presented opinion as fact.	☆	☆	☆	☆
I used half-truth.	☆	☆	☆	☆
I made my views clear and called for action.	☆	☆	☆	☆

Something I am especially pleased with

Something my audience liked in my writing

Something I'd like to do better next time

How to write answers to SATs questions

The SATs section in the pupil's book (pages 75–79) provides typical sample SATs questions to which you may or may not want children to write full answers. The main purpose is to give children practice in how to approach a SATs writing question.

Here is some guidance on using the section in the pupil's book:

- Choose one of the SATs questions to work on.
- Read through it together in class.
- Give children 5–10 minutes, in pairs, to brainstorm answers to the questions on the form on page 75.
- Go through the children's answers together.

The following pages include some pointers as to the sort of answers children should be expected to come up with. You can photocopy these and hand them out to children for revision purposes.

1–2 Story

Audience	No information given therefore assume teacher/marker
Purpose	To narrate imagined events To entertain, amuse or create suspense, etc.
Text type	Story – may be of particular genre
Structure	At least three main sections – beginning, middle, end Each section should be balanced
Sequencing and linking in the text	Chronological sequence (probably) Could include flashback or dual setting, etc.
Information and ideas	Use the ideas in the question as a starting point Write about how events make you feel
Language	Include some powerful verbs and interesting descriptive language
Star ways to impress the marker	★ Use paragraphs to set out ideas and events. ★ Make a short list of exciting/interesting words to use. ★ Use sentences of different types and lengths to vary the effect of the writing. ★ Use clear chronological connectives. ★ In the final paragraph, repeat some words/phrases from the beginning paragraph to bring the story 'full circle'.

3 Non-chronological report

Audience	Zxargian emperor
Purpose	To give information about the people on Earth
Text type	Report, non-chronological (mainly) Some explanation (possibly)
Structure	Definition Discrete sections of information (any number possible) Concluding section of particularly interesting facts
Sequencing and linking in the text	Any sensible order in main section Headings
Information and ideas	Appearance; homes; transport; hobbies; ways of behaving
Language	Formal – out of respect for emperor Impersonal – characteristic of text type General information – report is about *all* humans Present tense
Star ways to impress the marker	★ Use clear, helpful headings for sections of text. ★ Present some information in an alternative way, e.g. a bulleted list, a column, a table. ★ Use proper 'formal' words, e.g. *limbs* for arm and legs. ★ Include one or two comparisons/contrasts between Earthlings and Zxargians – a chance to make up a few interesting and unusual words and ideas to conclude the text.

4 Discussion and point of view – in letter form

Audience	Councillor Goodbody
Purpose	To set out a controversial issue To consider both sides To persuade reader towards own point of view
Text type	Discussion/persuasion Letter
Structure	Address, date and greeting Reason for writing Sequence of points relating to main issue State and justify own viewpoint Closing statement: urge the councillor to take action Closure
Sequencing and linking in the text	Connectives that show opposing views, e.g. *some people say… others, however, think…*
Information and ideas	See the pupil's book for ideas.
Language	Conventional letter opening Strong/persuasive Formal but personal
Star ways to impress the marker	★ Open with a characteristic structure that sets the tone clearly, e.g. *I am writing to you because…* ★ Close on a strong note, e.g. *I urge you to do the right thing by the community and…* ★ Use mature discussion language, e.g. *Of course, these people are entitled to their opinion. However…* ★ Use slightly weak language to consider the opposing viewpoint in a fair, but not very enthusiastic way. Use very strong and persuasive language to advance your own point of view! For example: *It is only fair to admit that a factory would provide some good jobs. On the other hand, the health risk to our community would be massive! The filthy smoke from the ugly factory chimneys could block out the sun and cause asthma in our children!*

5 Promotional leaflet

Audience	General public – anyone who might buy a holiday
Purpose	To advertise/promote Moondome To encourage/persuade holidaymakers to visit
Text type	Leaflet including information and promotional sections
Structure	Slogan/catchphrase – to get attention What and where Moondome is Description of attractions Final slogan
Sequencing and linking in the text	Use words and phrases to link persuasive points together, e.g. *furthermore, therefore, consequently.*
Information and ideas	See the pupil's book for ideas.
Language	Powerful, persuasive
Star ways to impress the marker	★ Make clear differences between different sections of the text – give clear, sensible information in some parts and use a persuasive style in others. ★ Use longer sentences and lots of interesting vocabulary in prose text sections; use 'snappy', poster-style language in others. ★ Use questions to involve the audience, e.g. *What will **you** do first at Moondome?* ★ Use alliteration, rhyme and other word-play to produce some 'catchy' headings for the persuasive sections. ★ Present some information in alternative ways, e.g. a brief timetable, bulleted lists of attractions.

6 Eyewitness report/recount

Audience	Self (assume teacher/marker)
Purpose	To retell 'real' experiences
Text type	Recount/journal
Structure	Orientation Events in time order Reorientation
Sequencing and linking in the text	Chronological order Time/sequential connectives
Information and ideas	Historical information Personal reactions/comments
Language	Past tense Historical words Personal, informal language
Star ways to impress the marker	★ Make a list of historical vocabulary to use, such as words for Tudor clothes or pastimes. ★ Use clear chronological connectives. ★ Include personal comments that express the horror of the occasion, e.g. *I could scarcely believe my eyes* or *The cries of the drowning men still echo in my ears.* ★ Change tense in the reorientation to bring the story up to the present and consider the future. For example: *It <u>was</u> a dreadful thing to witness. Today I <u>feel</u> quite shocked and distressed. The disastrous loss of that fine vessel, the beautiful Mary Rose, <u>will haunt</u> my dreams for many years to come.*

7 Information text

Audience	No information given therefore assume teacher/marker
Purpose	To inform, explain; to create interest/enthusiasm
Text type	Mixed – information, explanation, some persuasion (possibly)
Structure	Definition/introduction of subject Information sections Closing section
Sequencing and linking in the text	Subheadings Chronological connectives for explanations
Information and ideas	A hobby, sport or pet; a place you often visit
Language	Specific vocabulary relating to the topic Present tense verbs
Star ways to impress the marker	★ Mix personal and impersonal styles – a personal introduction stating why the subject is of special interest to you, how long you have been interested in it, etc. Share a few examples of your experience. Then switch into more formal, impersonal style to present aspects of information and explanation. ★ Use some powerful adjectives in writing about the topic. These will create interest and convey enthusiasm. ★ Use headings to organise and sequence separate sections of information/explanation. ★ Finish on a strong note, with a particularly interesting detail, a recommendation to readers or another personal viewpoint.

8 Explanation of a process

Audience	No information given therefore assume teacher/marker
Purpose	To explain a process To show sequence and relationship between steps/parts of the process
Text type	Explanation
Structure	Define/describe the process stage by stage – sequential
Sequencing and linking in the text	Begin at chosen point, follow process through Chronological sequence Demonstrate cause and effect
Information and ideas	See the pupil's book for information.
Language	Formal, impersonal Technical vocabulary relating to water cycle
Star ways to impress the marker	★ Make a list of scientific vocabulary to do with the water cycle. Use these words in your explanation. ★ Use clear headings – number them if appropriate. ★ Use a range of chronological connectives to sequence the stages in the process. ★ Use cause and effect connectives to show how different parts of the process relate to each other, e.g. *leads to, causes, has the effect of.*

Name .... Date ....

Read this scene from *Crummy Mummy and Me*.

Underline the **dialogue** in red.
Underline the **speech stage directions** in blue.
Underline the **action stage directions** in green.

When you have finished, act out the scene with your partner.

Minna	(*Sadly*) I don't feel well, Mum. In fact I feel truly terrible.
Mum	You don't look very poorly.
Minna	Well, I feel absolutely rotten.
Mum	You don't look it.
Minna	(*Crossly*) I'm sorry I can't manage a bright green face for you! Or purple spots on my belly! Or all my hair falling out! But I feel rotten just the same!

(Minna starts to cry.)

Mum	(*Putting her arms around Minna*) Now it's not like you to cry. You must be a little bit off today.
Minna	I'm not off! I'm not leftover milk or rotten fish.
Mum	(*Wiping Minna's eyes with a tissue*) There, there. Don't fret Minna. Don't get upset. You just hop straight back up those stairs like a good poppet, and in a minute I'll bring something nice up on a tray and you can have a quiet day in bed with Mum looking after you until you feel better.
Minna	Thanks Mum. I'll see you in a minute.

(Minna goes upstairs.)

Based on *Crummy Mummy and Me* by Anne Fine

Name ....

Date ....

Read this scene from *Crummy Mummy and Me*.
Write the **stage directions** for **speech** and **action** in the brackets.
Use the word bank in the pupil's book to help you.

When you have finished, act out the scene with your partner.

Minna (_____) I don't feel well, Mum. In fact I feel truly terrible.

Mum (_____) You don't look very poorly.

Minna Well, I feel absolutely rotten.

Mum You don't look it.

Minna (_____) I'm sorry I can't manage a bright green face for you! Or purple spots on my belly! Or all my hair falling out! But I feel rotten just the same!

(_____)

Mum (_____) Now it's not like you to cry. You must be a little bit off today.

Minna (_____) I'm not off! I'm not leftover milk or rotten fish.

Mum (_____) There, there. Don't fret Minna. Don't get upset. You just hop straight back up those stairs like a good poppet, and in a minute I'll bring something nice up on a tray and you can have a quiet day in bed with Mum looking after you until you feel better.

Minna Thanks Mum. I'll see you in a minute.

(_____)

Name .... Date ....

Complete this character profile for Crusher Maggot.

Name: Crusher Maggot
Age: 29
Appearance: _____
_____

Personality: _____
_____

Now add the dialogue and stage directions for Crusher in this scene.
When you have finished, act out the scene with your partner.

Someone has stolen Crusher's TV and video. Crusher is upset because he wanted to watch the snooker.

Crusher   Where's the telly and video?

Mum   (*Shouting*) Oh no! We've had burglars!

Crusher   (   ) _____

Mum   I know it was yours. I didn't ask them to take it, did I?

Crusher   (   ) _____

Mum   I didn't hear anything. I was in the kitchen.

Crusher   (   ) _____

Mum   Never mind about the snooker, we'd better call the police.

Crusher   (   ) _____

Based on *Crummy Mummy and Me* by Anne Fine

Name .... Date ....

Beginning
Problem (Scene one)

Middle
Event (Scene two)

Event (Scene three)

Conflict/climax (Scene four)

End
Resolution (Scene five)

Name .... Date ....

Title

Scene 1
Setting

Characters

Action

Scene 2
Setting

Characters

Action

Scene 3
Setting

Characters

Action

Scene 4
Setting

Characters

Action

Name .... Date ....

Play evaluation sheet

Title _____
Star rating _____
Comments _____
_____

Plot

We liked _____
_____

It could be improved by _____
_____

Characters

We liked _____
_____

They could be
improved by _____
_____

Setting – props, music, costumes, lighting (if used)

We liked _____
_____

It could be improved by _____
_____

Performance – actions, expression, pace of scenes

We liked _____
_____

It could be improved by _____
_____

Star ratings	
*	fair
**	good
***	very good
****	brilliant

Name ....

Date ....

Title _____

Author _____

Date started _____

Date completed _____

Before I read the book, I thought it would be about _____

_____

_____

Characters

I liked _____

_____

_____

_____

I didn't like _____

_____

_____

_____

I would change _____

_____

_____

_____

Words which I found interesting or unusual

Name ....   Date ....

Read this recount.

When you have finished, draw boxes around the **orientation**,
events and **reorientation**. Label these sections.

By 215 BC Rome had grown from a handful of villages to become the most
powerful city in Italy, and was developing ambitions to build an empire. For a
few years, however, the genius of the Greek philosopher Archimedes kept
them at bay.

First of all, the Romans attacked the rich Greek city of Syracuse in Sicily,
which lay to the south of Italy. In response, Archimedes invented a massive
catapult, which shot huge stones at the Roman army and ships so they could
not get near to the city walls. Archimedes's catapults kept the Romans out of
Syracuse for three years.

Then, in 213 BC, Archimedes came up with another invention to halt the
Roman advance. He set up large mirrors along the harbour walls, which
reflected the sun on to nearby Roman ships and set them on fire.

By 211 BC, however, the Romans finally broke through the Greek defences and
brought terror to the citizens of Syracuse. Archimedes was killed by a Roman
soldier.

It was the beginning of the end for the Greeks. In the space of twenty years, all
Greek cities had been conquered by the unstoppable Roman war machine.

Now draw up a grid like this for the recount. Fill in the **key points** only.

Who?	What?	Where?	When?	Why?	How?

Name .... Date ....

Headline _____

Orientation

Picture

Caption

Main events

Reorientation

Name ....

Date ....

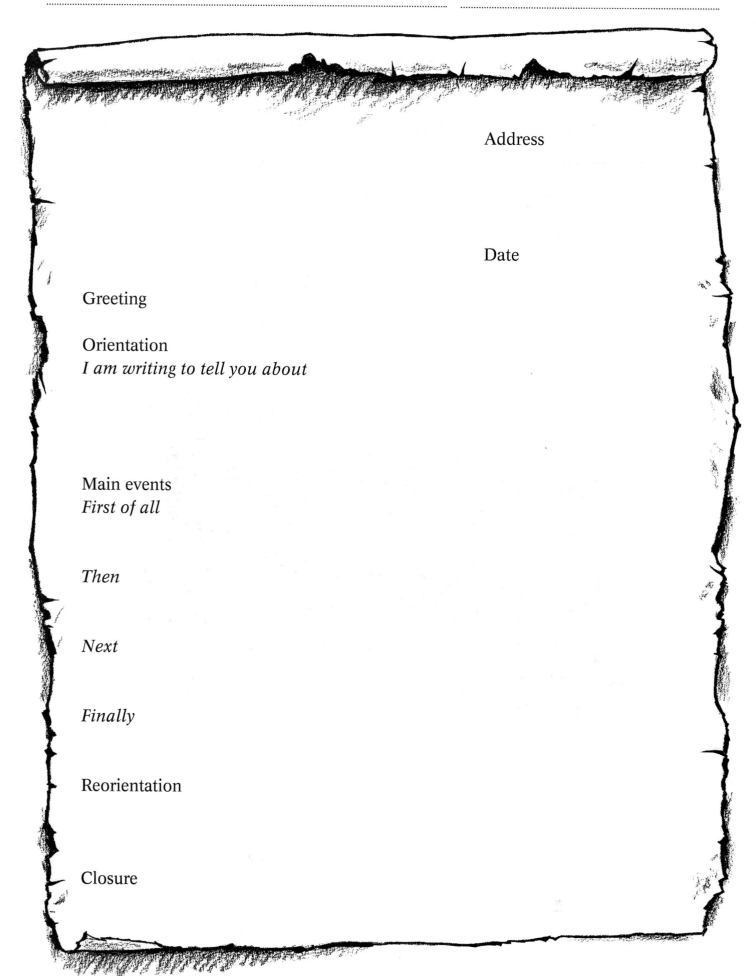

Address

Date

Greeting

Orientation
I am writing to tell you about

Main events
First of all

Then

Next

Finally

Reorientation

Closure

Name

Date

How to make a Greek pinhole camera

1   Make a box of black card, 20 x 10 x 10 cm.

2   Make a small pinhole in black paper at one end.

3   Place grease-proof paper across the other end.

4   Hold it up to a bright scene.

5   The scene will be 'projected' on to the grease-proof paper.

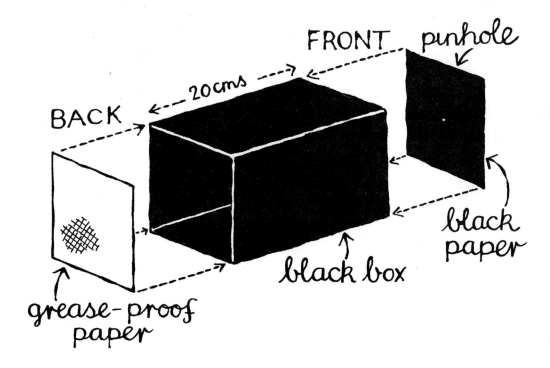

FRONT   pinhole

BACK

20cms

black paper

black box

grease-proof paper

© Cambridge University Press 2001

Name .... Date ....

These pictures and sentences from 'Odysseus and the Cyclops' are in the wrong order.
Cut them out and rearrange them correctly.

Odysseus and his men escaped from the
Cyclops by hiding under his sheep.

The Cyclops sat blocking the way out
of the cave.

Odysseus and his men were trapped in
the cave.

While the Cyclops lay asleep, the Greeks
blinded him with a huge spear.

Name .... Date ....

Think of an extraordinary character for your legend.
Make notes of its features in this table.

Size	Strange features	Sounds	Actions	Powers

Now think of a **setting** where your character lives. Write your ideas here:

This place is _____
_____
_____

I can see _____
_____
_____

I can hear _____
_____
_____

I can smell _____
_____

This place makes me feel _____
_____

Name

Date

Beginning

My hero/heroine is called

My extraordinary character is

This character lives in

This place suits the character because

The problem for my hero/heroine is

Middle

Event 1

Event 2

Event 3

Climax

End

The problem is resolved because

The conclusion is

Name ....

Date ....

(Address)

(Greeting)

(Message)

(Closure)

Name ....

Date ....

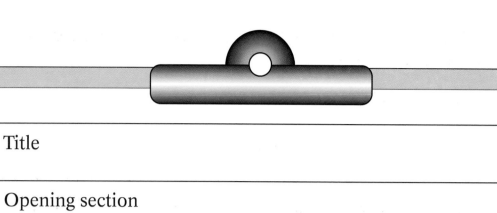

Title

Opening section

Main section
(with headings, sub-headings and bullet points)

Closing section

Sources   Glossary

Name

Date

Cut this sheet along the dotted lines and group the statements into sections according to the three-part framework.

Divide the main section into logical paragraphs.

The planets

Venus is often called the Morning or Evening Star, depending on when it is visible.	Earth's atmosphere is rich in oxygen.
There are nine major planets in our solar system.	A planet is a large celestial body that orbits a star.
The inner planets are all small and rocky.	Mars is called the 'red planet'.
The mountains on Mars are coloured by red iron 'rust'.	Venus has a carbon dioxide atmosphere 90 times thicker than Earth's.
Mercury, the nearest planet to the Sun, has an atmosphere of sodium and potassium.	There is water on much of the surface of Earth.
Mars has a cold atmosphere of carbon dioxide.	There may once have been water on Mars.
The inner planets, lying closest to the Sun, are Mercury, Venus, Earth and Mars.	None of the planets, with the exception of Earth, is capable of supporting life.
Earth's weather systems create areas with hot, cold and moderate climates.	The dusty surface of Mercury is pitted with craters caused by asteroid strikes.

Name

Date

Here are 18 extra facts that go with the ones on copymaster 17. Cut this sheet along the dotted lines, and organise all the facts into a logical order. Find the **key words** in each section and write in some **headings**.

More about the planets

Helium and hydrogen are the main gases on Jupiter.	Jupiter is the largest planet in the solar system.
Gas clouds on Jupiter are coloured and swirling.	Saturn's most famous feature is its planetary rings.
Scientists think that life may develop on Jupiter in the distant future.	The surface of Jupiter cannot be seen beneath gas clouds.
Saturn is the second largest planet in the solar system.	Pluto is very cold.
Saturn is a cold gas giant made of hydrogen, helium, methane and ammonia.	Uranus is made of helium, hydrogen and methane.
The methane in Neptune's atmosphere gives the planet its colour.	The outer planets are large balls of rock, liquid and gas.
Uranus has a pale green atmosphere.	The methane in Pluto's atmosphere freezes and forms polar ice-caps.
Neptune has the highest winds in the solar system.	Pluto is yellowish in colour.
Lying furthest from the Sun are Jupiter, Saturn, Uranus, Neptune and Pluto, known as the outer planets.	Neptune is blue.

Name .... Date ....

The Adventures of Isabel

Isabel met an enormous bear,
Isabel, Isabel didn't care.
The bear was hungry, the bear was ravenous,
The bear's big mouth was cruel and cavernous.
The bear said, Isabel, glad to meet you,
How do, Isabel, now I'll eat you!
Isabel, Isabel didn't worry,
Isabel didn't scream or scurry,
She washed her hands and she straightened her hair up,
Then Isabel quietly ate the bear up.

Once in a night as black as pitch
Isabel met a wicked witch.
The witch's face was cross and wrinkled,
The witch's gums with teeth were sprinkled.
Ho ho, Isabel! the old witch crowed,
I'll turn you into an ugly toad!
Isabel, Isabel didn't worry,
Isabel didn't scream or scurry,
She showed no rage, she showed no rancour,
But she turned the witch into milk and drank her!

Isabel met a hideous giant,
Isabel continued self-reliant.
The giant was hairy, the giant was horrid,
He had one eye in the middle of his forehead.
Good morning, Isabel, the giant said,
I'll grind your bones to make my bread.
Isabel, Isabel didn't worry,
Isabel didn't scream or scurry,
She nibbled the zwieback that she always fed off,
And when it was gone, she cut the giant's head off.

From 'The Adventures of Isabel' by Ogden Nash

Name ....

Date ....

Key features of performance poetry	Tick if you find an example in the poem.	Examples from the poem: _____ _____	Examples from the poem: _____ _____	Examples from the poem: _____ _____
Rhythm: a strong beat, easy to clap out				
Rhyme: simple repetitive scheme				
Repetition: repeated words and phrases				
Use of direct speech, dialogue				
Direct address to the audience				

Name .... Date ....

Jim

He hadn't gone a yard when – Bang!
With open jaws a lion sprang,
And hungrily began to eat
The boy: beginning at his feet.

Now, just imagine how it feels
When first your toes and then your heels,
And then by gradual degrees,
Your shins and ankles, calves and knees,
Are slowly eaten, bit by bit.
No wonder Jim detested it!
No wonder that he shouted "Hi!"
The honest keeper heard his cry,
Though very fat he almost ran
To help the little gentleman.
"Ponto!" he ordered as he came
(for Ponto was the lion's name),
"Ponto" he cried, with angry frown.
"Let go, Sir! Down, Sir! Put it down!"

From 'Jim' by Hilaire Belloc

The Charge of the Light Brigade

Half a league, half a league,
Half a league onward,
All in the valley of Death
Rode the six hundred.
"Forward, the Light Brigade!
Charge for the guns!" he said:
Into the valley of Death
Rode the six hundred.

Cannon to right of them
Cannon to left of them,
Cannon in front of them
Volley'd and thunder'd;
Storm'd at with shot and shell,
Boldly they rode and well,
Into the jaws of Death,
Into the mouth of Hell
Rode the six hundred.

From 'The Charge of the Light Brigade' by Lord Tennyson

Name ....

Date ....

The Song of Hiawatha

Then Iagoo, the great boaster,
He the marvellous story-teller,
He the traveller and the talker,
He the friend of old Nokomis,
Made a bow for Hiawatha;
From a branch of ash he made it,
From an oak-bough made the arrows,
Tipped with flint, and winged with feathers,
And the cord he made of deer-skin.
Then he said to Hiawatha:
"Go, my son, into the forest,
Where the red-deer herd together,
Kill for us a famous roebuck,
Kill for us a deer with antlers!"

From 'The Song of Hiawatha' by Henry Longfellow

Horatius

XX
Just then a scout came flying,
All wild with haste and fear:
"To arms! To arms! Sir Consul;
Lars Porsena is here."
On the low hills to westward,
The Consul fixed his eye,
And saw the swarthy storm of dust
Rise fast along the sky.

XXI
And nearer fast and nearer
Doth the red whirlwind come;
And louder still and still more loud,
From underneath that rolling cloud,
Is heard the trumpet's war-note proud,
The trampling, and the hum.
And plainly and more plainly
Now through the gloom appears,
Far to left and far to right,
In broken gleams of dark-blue light,
The long array of helmets bright
The long array of spears.

From 'The Lays of Ancient Rome' by Thomas Macaulay

The Camel

The camel has a single hump;
The dromedary, two;
Or else the other way around.
I'm never sure. Are you?

Ogden Nash

Name ....   Date ....

Book title	Author

END OF CHAPTER 1		**HALF-WAY THROUGH**
Main characters		
Brief description	How they might change	My view now
Plot		
Story so far	What I think will happen	What has happened

END OF BOOK: RESOLUTION

I thought the ending of this book was _____
because

Name .... Date ....

George is trying to persuade his mum to let him have a pet snake.
Act out the conversation with your partner. Take it in turns to be George.
You must reply to Mum's questions with a reason and supporting evidence.
The first one has been done for you.

You're not having a snake. You'll never clean out its tank.

Snakes don't need their tanks cleaned out very often because they don't make much mess. When it does need cleaning out, I'll do it because it is my pet.

How can I be sure you'll feed it every day?

Snakes shouldn't be living in tanks. It's cruel. They need lots of space.

What about when it gets ill? How can I trust you to look after it then?

Name ....

Date ....

This is the transcript of a radio interview with a football fan
who believes that footballers are paid too much.

Some of the persuasive and linking words are missing. Work as
a group to choose the best words to fill the gaps.

"I believe that footballers should be paid less money.
_____ players work hard, training throughout the year and playing
more than one match per week. _____, this cannot be seen as hard
work. There are many people like doctors and nurses who work far longer hours
than this for a lot less money.

_____ players do bring in money for the club. _____,
this money should be spent on community projects and relieving some of the
suffering of poor people. Why should hundreds of people live on the streets while
footballers own at least three houses each? _____, the money could be
used to reduce the price of tickets to football matches which are so expensive that
many people cannot afford to go and watch their favourite team play.

_____ players should be paid less and the money put towards
helping people in need."

Can you think of other points to add to the argument?
Write them down, remembering to use persuasive and linking words.

Name
....

Date
....

Pretend that you own a snake. You have written a letter to the
newspaper about keeping exotic pets.

Write **your address**, the **date** and a **greeting** and **closure** in the boxes.
Draw a box around each paragraph in the main part of the letter.
Label each paragraph using a title from this list:

- Capturing animals
- Conclusion (summary + action)
- Inspections
- Introduction (state position)
- Looking after animals

The Editor,
Cardiff Daily Post,
63–66 St James Gardens,
Cardiff
CR12 6XE

I am writing to support the opening of 'Ed's Exotic Pets'. Exotic animals are very
interesting to keep and they are easy to look after.

Animals are not hurt when they are captured and they are given food and water for the
journey. Lots of animals that are in danger of becoming extinct in the wild can be
looked after and bred in captivity. Surely everyone must see that this is a good thing?

Pet shops are inspected every year and inspectors can check that animals are well
looked after. What is more, pet shops have to apply for a licence before they can open
and the animals' cages are checked to see that they have enough room to move about.

Some owners cannot look after exotic animals but most people can. Owners give them
the right food and enough space and the animals are happy.

Therefore, 'Ed's Exotic Pets' should be allowed to open and I urge people not to sign
the petition outside the shop.

Name ....   Date ....

Cut out the sections of this letter and put them in the right order. Then read through the letter with your partner to check it makes sense.

Furthermore, most people are perfectly capable of looking after exotic animals. They understand their diet and provide them with enough space to live in. Of course, there are a few cases of neglect and cruelty, but there are also thousands of exotic pets who are well cared for and live happily with their owners.

Yours faithfully,
    Mr A. Zindani

---

23 Willow Drive,
Rossington,
CR76 2SA

The Editor,
Cardiff Daily Post,
63–66 St James Gardens,
Cardiff,
CR12 6XE

Therefore, 'Ed's Exotic Pets' should be allowed to open. The pets will be well cared for by the shop and by the people who buy them. I believe that people should be allowed to keep whatever pet they choose.

I urge your readers not to sign the petition outside the shop, and to look around at the wonderful range of animals that it is now possible to keep.

10th June 2001

Firstly, exotic animals are transported according to regulations and are given enough space and adequate food and water. They are carefully captured and many endangered animals are then bred in captivity to ensure that the species survives. Surely this is conservation, not destruction?

Dear Sir/Madam

I am writing to support the opening of the new pet shop 'Ed's Exotic Pets'. The real truth is that exotic animals are well looked after by pet shops and owners and they make wonderful pets. Owning an exotic pet definitely impresses your friends.

Secondly, environmental health officers inspect pet shops every year to check that the animals have suitable living conditions. What is more, pet shop owners have to apply for licences before they can sell exotic animals. These controls ensure that animals in pet shops are well cared for.

Name

Date

Para. 1
Purpose and position

Para. 2
Argument 1

Para. 3
Argument 2

Para. 4
Argument 3

Para. 5
Summary and action

PUBLISHED BY THE PRESS SYNDICATE OF THE UNIVERSITY OF CAMBRIDGE
The Pitt Building, Trumpington Street, Cambridge, United Kingdom

CAMBRIDGE UNIVERSITY PRESS
The Edinburgh Building, Cambridge CB2 2RU, UK
40 West 20th Street, New York, NY 10011-4211, USA
10 Stamford Road, Oakleigh, VIC 3166, Australia
Ruiz de Alarcón 13, 28014 Madrid, Spain
Dock House, The Waterfront, Cape Town 8001, South Africa

http://www.cambridge.org

First published 2001
Reprinted 2001

Printed in the United Kingdom by GreenShires Group Ltd, Kettering, Northamptonshire.

Typefaces Concorde, Frutiger, ITC Kabel   *System* QuarkXPress®

A catalogue record for this book is available from the British Library

ISBN 0 521 80550 3

Cover design by Traffika Publishing Ltd
Design by Peter Simmonett and Angela Ashton
Artwork chosen by Heather Richards
Illustrations by Peter Bailey, Beccy Blake, Lizzie Finlay/Heather Richards, John Holder,
Sally Kindberg, Ed McLachlan/Folio, Specs Art, Stella Voce/Heather Richards

We would like to thank the following teachers and headteachers for their help on Cornerstones for
Writing: Anne Allen, Lorna Ferry, Bonnie Kennedy, Jackie Lucas, Carol Meek and Susan Seed.

We are grateful to the following for permission to reproduce text extracts:
Crummy Mummy and Me, Anne Fine, 1988, published by Penguin Books Ltd, reproduced by
permission of David Higham Associates; 'How to make a Greek pinhole camera', Terry Deary, 1996,
from *The Groovy Greeks* (Scholastic Children's Books); 'The Adventures of Isabel' and 'The Camel'
by Ogden Nash (Little, Brown and Company Inc.); 'Jim' by Hilaire Belloc, reprinted by permission of
The Peters Fraser and Dunlop Group Limited on behalf of The Estate of Hilaire Belloc.

Every effort has been made to trace all copyright holders. If there are any outstanding copyright issues
of which we are unaware, please contact Cambridge University Press.